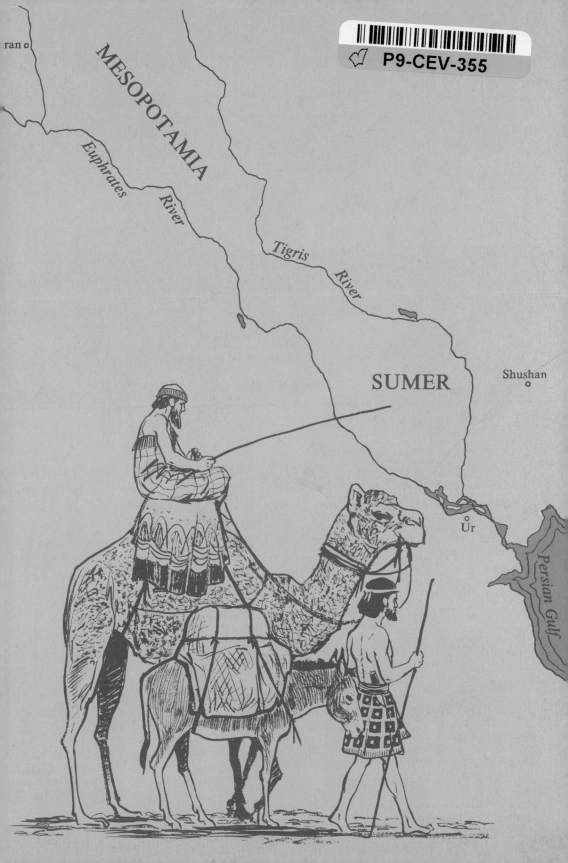

MESOPOTAMIA

Euphrates River

Tigris River

SUMER

Shushan

Ur

Persian Gulf

ran

THEY
TRUSTED
GOD

THEY TRUSTED GOD

BIBLE STORIES RETOLD
by Aylesa Forsee

Illustrations by Hank Ziol

The Christian Science Publishing Society
Boston, Massachusetts, U.S.A.

Library of Congress Catalog Card Number: 79–90565

ISBN: 0–87510–122–4

© 1980 The Christian Science Publishing Society

Printed in the United States of America

CONTENTS

INTRODUCTION

The Bible is beautiful literature, fascinating history, and stirring drama. But more than this, it has been read and cherished through the centuries for the basic reason it was written: inspiration.

They trusted God is about Old Testament characters and their response to God's direction. The early Hebrews were led—both literally and figuratively—by the patriarchs Abraham and Jacob. They were later brought out of bondage in Egypt and into Canaan by Moses and Joshua. Fortified with the law—the Commandments—they settled into the land and after a while Ruth, a Moabite woman, came to live among them.

Then the Hebrew people were guided by the great prophet Samuel and ushered into nationhood under King David and King Solomon. Much later Nehemiah, a Jew living in Persia, showed his love for his people and for God by coming to rebuild the walls and the morale of Jerusalem.

In presenting these stories the author and editors hope to make the reader aware of Bible characters as actual people and to stir curiosity about the Bible as a whole.

Although plots, description, and chronology have been simplified, the stories are retold without interpretation. An occasional explanation or scholar's bit of historical information has been inserted, but special care has been taken to follow the Scriptures as closely as possible.

For some of the dialogue and in those passages where God is reported as speaking, the author has used the actual wording of the King James Version of the Bible. References are given at the end of each chapter.

One recurring theme of the Bible is that mankind's search for God coincides with God's plan. *They trusted God* illustrates how God revealed Himself through His people, sometimes in spite of their shortcomings, but always in a way that they were able to understand.

ABRAHAM

Abram, later called Abraham,
lived almost as many years before
the birth of Jesus as we live after it.
Abram was born at Ur, near the
Persian Gulf, but with his family and his
father Terah he had come on foot northward
up the Euphrates River Valley to Haran.

Today, Haran, which is in Turkey,
still has some huts much like those
Abram might have lived in. Many of the
people wear robes similar to those he
must have worn. Outside the city where
grapes, olives, and barley grew, Abram
tended his flocks.

After he became head of his branch of
the family, Abram followed God's instructions
to go to a new land. He and his family,
including his nephew Lot, traveled along
caravan routes south to the land of
Canaan on the sea we now call the
Mediterranean.

PIONEER IN FAITH

Abram stood outside his tent and watched the sun rise over the city of Haran nearby. Today he would begin a great adventure. Already his servants, herdsmen, and their families hurried and scurried, getting ready to travel.

After his father Terah died, Abram had prayed to God for guidance. "Leave this country and your own people," God told him. "Go to a land that I will show you. I will make of you a great nation."

Abram didn't even know what God meant. Yet he was ready to obey. At his side he would have his wife, Sarai, and his fatherless nephew, Lot. Lot would be second-in-command.

Finally Abram and the others were ready to leave. Tents, clothing, cooking pots, everything needed, was loaded on donkeys. Abram's brother, Nahor, other relatives, and friends came to say goodbye.

The herdsmen and shepherds moved off with bleating sheep and other animals. A few people mounted asses. Most would walk. Ahead might lie loneliness, wild animals, robbers. But there could be no turning back now. Abram drew his head-covering closer to shade his eyes.

Lot took his wife and family, his servants, flocks, and herds to a place near the city of Sodom.

After Lot was gone, the Lord told Abram, "Look out from where you are to the north and the south and the east and the west. All the land that you see I will give you and your descendants for ever."

Abram was grateful for God's promise, although still puzzled by the thought of descendants.

But at the moment what he needed most was to find grass for the animals. He moved to the plain of Mamre.

One day a messenger came running up to Abram's tent. "Armies have invaded our land," he said breathlessly. "They have plundered Sodom and Gomorrah. Lot is a prisoner."

Abram thanked the man and then made plans. He had no wish to fight. But the invaders must be driven out. And Lot must be rescued.

People with animals to protect always had some weapons, so Abram got these together and armed his servants and shepherds. With his little band of several hundred men, Abram set off after the enemy. Meanwhile, the invaders, slowed by prisoners and the loot they had taken, settled down at a place called Hobah for the night.

Abram and his men took the sleepy guards by surprise. The foreign army fled. Abram freed the prisoners, including Lot. Then he had all the stolen goods loaded to take back.

As Abram and his men returned from the rout, the king of Salem, Melchizedek, came out to meet them. Melchizedek, who was a priest as well as a king, had brought food. "The blessing of God be upon you, Abram," he said. "And blessed be God."

The king of Sodom also came to Abram. "Just give me

back my people who were captured," he said. "Keep what our enemy stole from my city."

"The food for my men, I'll accept," Abram answered. "But I will not keep one thread or sandal strap from anything of yours."

Abram went back to his quiet life at Mamre. He had flocks, herds, a loving and helpful wife, the respect of kings as well as of followers. Only one thing kept him from being completely happy. He longed for a son.

Among his people the main purpose of marriage was to have children. To die without a son was a dishonor. Sarai too felt disgraced because they had no children.

Many years passed. One day the Lord again appeared to Abram. "I am the Almighty God," He said. "Walk before me and be perfect. You shall be the father of many nations. Your name shall no longer be Abram but Abraham. And do not call your wife Sarai anymore. Call her Sarah."

A change of name was fairly common, but usually it marked some great happening in a person's life. What was the change this time? It might have been because Abraham worshiped only one God.

Then the Lord told Abraham, "Sarah shall bear you a son, and you will call him Isaac, and I will establish my covenant with him and his children."

Abraham had a hard time believing this. Through trust in God he had become a leader. God had protected him and his family. But he and Sarah were much too old to have children. The thought made him laugh.

One hot day, Abraham was sitting at the door of his tent on the plain of Mamre. When he looked up he saw three men and ran to meet them.

"Sirs," he said, "stop here and rest. I will bring water to

wash your feet. And I will bring bread for you to eat."

"Do as you have said," the men answered.

After the three men had eaten the bread and meat Abraham brought them, he once more heard the Lord speaking to him. "Sarah thy wife shall have a son."

By now Abraham was beginning to believe that God could do anything. But Sarah, who was in the tent behind him, laughed to herself. "Shall I have a son when I am old and my husband is old?"

Then the Lord said to Abraham, "Why did Sarah laugh? Is anything too hard for the Lord?"

These words stayed with Abraham long after the three men left. In due time, a son was born to Sarah and Abraham. They named him Isaac which means "one laughs." Sarah said, "God has made me laugh so that everyone who hears of it will laugh with me."

No parents ever loved a child more. As Isaac grew older, Abraham taught him how to use a sheepskin for a water bag, how to care for sheep. Above all he taught him to love God.

One day Abraham heard the voice of the Lord telling him, "Take now your only son, Isaac, and go to the land of Moriah. There offer him for a burnt offering."

Abraham lived among the Canaanites, who believed in sacrifices to win the favor of their gods. To show their faith and obedience they would offer whatever was dearest to them—sometimes even an oldest son. This influenced Abraham.

He had always tried to obey the Lord, but this seemed a terrible command. And always before what the Lord had asked of Abraham seemed understandable, even good. Giving up Isaac, his only son, didn't seem good at all!

Still Abraham felt he should trust and do what the Lord had asked.

Next morning Abraham had servants prepare goods and provisions for the journey to Moriah. After he saddled his ass he called Isaac to him. "We are going on a journey together," he said.

Three days later they came to the place where Abraham thought he should build an altar. He put wood on it, ready for a fire. Then he bound Isaac and laid him on the wood.

At that moment Abraham heard a voice saying, "Abraham, don't hurt the lad. Now I know for sure that you love God most of all."

Joyfully Abraham freed Isaac. Now he understood that his God did not really ask for the sacrifice of a son. But Abraham had in his way shown his love for and trust in God. Abraham's children and grandchildren and great-grand-children would be blessed and would be as many as the stars in the sky.

In the years that followed, Abraham became a respected leader. He was spoken of as the father of the Hebrew nation. Even today Abraham is remembered as a man who dared to trust God, a pioneer in faith.

The story is found in Genesis, chapters 12 through 22.

JACOB

When Isaac was forty years
old, his father, Abraham, arranged
a marriage for him with Rebekah.
For many years they had no children.
Isaac, who had learned as a child
to trust God, prayed. At last Rebekah
gave birth—to twins. They named
the boys Esau and Jacob.

Isaac was successful as a herdsman
and a farmer. He sometimes had troubles
to settle with neighbors who tried
to take over the wells that he and Abraham
had dug. But the more important struggle
that touched Isaac's life was the rivalry between
Esau and Jacob. Rebekah loved Jacob
the most while Isaac favored Esau,
who was the first-born son.

BROTHERS AND BLESSINGS

Jacob and Esau were twins, but they didn't look alike or think alike. They didn't even do many of the same things.

Esau, a desert hunter, went off for days at a time to track down birds and beasts. Usually, Jacob stayed close to the tents where his parents lived at Beersheba in Canaan. He worked with the flocks and herds of his father, Isaac.

As the twins grew to manhood, Jacob was sometimes jealous of his brother. Esau had been born only moments before Jacob. Yet Esau had all the privileges of the oldest son, because of his birthright.

That meant he would inherit a double share of his father's vast flocks and herds—whatever Isaac owned. Jacob wanted those things, too.

His mother, Rebekah, was eager to see Jacob get ahead. Before the twins were born, God had spoken to her saying, "The elder shall serve the younger."

But Rebekah didn't see how this was going to happen, since Esau had the birthright. And Esau was the favorite of their father, Isaac. Esau had skill as a hunter. Isaac liked the tasty venison dish Esau made for him.

One day at mealtime Jacob got some lentils. With these he made a stew and cooked it in a pot over an open fire. The lentils were almost done when Jacob saw Esau coming from the hunt.

Esau was not taking big, quick steps the way he usually did. And he had no game. Esau came over and sniffed the aroma of the stew.

"Give me some of the red pottage," he said. "I'm starved."

A sly thought came to Jacob. "What will you give for it?" he asked.

"Anything."

"Would you trade your rights as eldest son?" asked Jacob.

"I'm starving," said Esau. "What good is a birthright if I die of hunger?"

"Swear that the birthright is mine," Jacob insisted.

"I swear," said Esau. "Now give me the food."

Esau ate the stew. Then he went off acting as if he didn't care at all that he had sold his birthright.

Years passed. Jacob did not marry. But Esau, as the custom was, had several wives.

Later on, Isaac began to lose his sight. He began to think about how old he was becoming.

One day Rebekah called to Jacob, "Come quickly."

"What is it?" asked Jacob.

"I overheard your father talking to Esau," she said. "He has sent him to get some game and make a venison stew for him. Then he plans to give Esau his blessing."

Such a blessing, customarily given by an aged father to his oldest son, would supposedly bring health, peace, prosperity, wisdom, and victory in battle. Jacob felt he needed that blessing to make his birthright complete.

Rebekah had a plan for Jacob to get the blessing. "Now do exactly as I tell you," she said. "Go out and get two of the young goats from the flock before Esau gets back. I'll make a tasty dish out of them for your father. After he has eaten it, he will bless you instead of Esau. He can't see well enough to know which one of you is with him."

"Mother!" said Jacob. "He won't be fooled that easily. He's sure to touch me. He'll know I'm not Esau. Esau is hairy. And when he finds out I'm fooling him, he will curse me instead of bless me."

"Let the curse be on me," said Rebekah.

Jacob did as his mother told him. Rebekah cooked the meat with onions and herbs. Then she handed Jacob clothes belonging to Esau. They smelled of wild things and of the outdoors.

"Put these on," she told Jacob. "Your father can't see. But these clothes have Esau's scent."

Jacob changed clothes. Then Rebekah tied goatskins on his arms and hands.

"Now go," she told him.

Jacob's heart beat fast as he took the bread and steaming meat to his father's tent. "I'm here, Father," he said.

"Are you Jacob or Esau?" Isaac asked.

"I am Esau," lied Jacob. "I did as you told me. Now sit up and eat. Then you can bless me."

"How did you find game so quickly, my son?" Isaac asked.

Jacob hesitated. He wasn't going to be able to stop with one lie. "Your God put it in my path," he told Isaac.

"Come here," his father said. "I want to feel you to be sure you are Esau."

Jacob went over to him. Isaac felt Jacob's hands.

"The voice is Jacob's," Isaac said, puzzled. "But the hands are Esau's."

Once more, still sounding doubtful, he said, "Are you really Esau?"

"Yes, of course," said Jacob.

"Then bring me the venison."

Isaac ate the meat. Then he said, "Come here and kiss me, Son."

As Jacob did this, Isaac got a whiff of the borrowed clothing. "The smell is like the smell of a field which the Lord has blessed," he said. "May God always give you plenty of rain for your crops and good harvest of grain. Let people serve you, and nations bow down to you. Be the master of your brothers. . . ."

Jacob now had his father's blessing. Nobody could take it from him; it was not possible for his father to take it back.

As Jacob was leaving the tent, he heard Esau coming in from the hunt. Esau cooked venison and took it to his father. There he found he had been tricked. Esau was disappointed and furious. Isaac was very upset and also very sad. But Isaac did promise Esau he would not always have to serve Jacob.

A short time later, Rebekah told Jacob, "I have heard that your brother Esau is saying, 'My father will die soon. Then I will kill Jacob!' "

Overcome by fear, Jacob stood speechless.

Rebekah wanted to arrange things. "Go to my brother Laban, in Haran, in the land of Padan-aram," she told Jacob. "Stay there until your brother is no longer angry."

Before Jacob could think of what to do next, Rebekah went off to Isaac's tent to persuade him to send Jacob away to find a wife. Her argument was that it wouldn't be

suitable for him to marry a local Canaanite woman. These women worshiped idols instead of the one true God. In a short time Rebekah came out and told Jacob his father wanted to see him.

"Your mother has been here," Isaac said. "We have decided we do not want you to marry one of the Canaanite women. Instead, go at once to your uncle. Marry one of Laban's daughters. God bless you as He did your grandfather, Abraham, to whom He gave this land."

Rebekah got some food and things together for Jacob. "I will send for you as soon as Esau forgets what has happened," she told him.

Jacob's moments of jealousy, ambition, and lies had grieved his father, and made Esau hate him. He was going to have to leave his family, his own land. What good was the blessing now?

A few nights after he left Beersheba, Jacob came to a bare, rocky place. He heard no familiar sounds or voices. There were no good smells of food cooking.

Jacob was alone. At bedtime he took a rock for a pillow and lay down on the hard ground. Wind rustled among the few dry brambles.

Finally Jacob slept. He dreamed that he saw a great ladder. Its feet rested on the earth, but it reached up to the sky. Angels went up and down the ladder.

In his dream Jacob heard a voice saying, "I am the God of Abraham and of your father, Isaac. The ground you are lying on is yours. I will give it to you and your descendants. What's more, I am with you. I will watch over you wherever you go. And I will bring you safely to this land."

When Jacob woke from the dream, he could hardly shake it off. "Surely the Lord is in this place, and I knew it not," he said.

In a way the dream comforted him. But it also made Jacob uneasy. He remembered his lies and trickery. Jacob had not expected Isaac's God to be with him or to speak to him. Now it seemed that the God of Abraham and Isaac was *his* God too! And God was *here* with him.

Now the place seemed holy to Jacob. He wanted to do something to honor it. Jacob picked up the stone he had used for a pillow and set it up as a kind of symbol of the presence of God. He poured some oil over the stone. "I shall call this place Bethel," he said. Bethel meant "the house of God."

Now Jacob began to think about God—His presence and power. He vowed: "If God will be with me, keep me safe, give me food and clothes so that I come again to my father's house in peace; then shall the Lord be my God."

It was time for Jacob to move on. A long journey still lay ahead of him. He didn't know what life would be like at his uncle's place in a new land. But Jacob had begun to learn that he couldn't get away from God and God's purpose for him, whether at home or in a strange land.

TRIALS AND TRICKERY

From Bethel, Jacob traveled toward Haran. At times he came to places where there were olive groves, vineyards, and fertile plains. But he also crossed deserts and climbed mountains.

Near walled cities, Jacob saw many people and met caravans of travelers. But some days he had no company except swallows, glossy ravens, or cranes with tails of drooping black feathers.

Late one morning Jacob got to a place where fig and olive trees grew. Ahead he saw a bit more green than usual. Soon he heard voices and the bleating of sheep. As he got closer he saw shepherds and their flocks resting around a well.

Jacob walked over to the shepherds. "Friends," he said, "where are you from?"

"Haran," one of them told him.

"Do you know a man named Laban?" asked Jacob.

"He lives near here," one of the shepherds said. "Look! There comes his daughter Rachel with her father's sheep."

Even from a distance Jacob could tell that Rachel was beautiful. The sheep looked healthy. Laban must be very rich. While he waited, Jacob talked with the shepherds.

When Rachel got to the well, Jacob went over and rolled away the heavy stone covering the mouth of the well. While she watched in surprise he began filling the trough so the sheep could drink. Then Jacob turned to Rachel and kissed her.

"You are my cousin," he explained. "I am Rebekah's son Jacob."

"I must tell my father," said Rachel. She ran away quickly.

Will Laban be pleased to see me? Jacob wondered as he watched Rachel running toward her father's home. Soon Laban came hurrying toward him. "Stay with us and be welcome," he said, putting his arm around him.

Jacob enjoyed his visit. Although a guest, he worked in the fields and tended his uncle's flocks.

After Jacob had been there a month, his uncle said, "You don't need to work without pay just because you are a relative. How much do you want?"

Jacob didn't really want money. He wanted Rachel. He had loved her from the moment he saw her. But he was not able to pay for her in gifts as was the custom. "I'll work for you seven years, if you'll give me Rachel as my wife," he offered.

"Agreed," said Laban. "Better for her to marry you than someone outside the family."

Because Jacob cared for Rachel so much, the seven years seemed short. At the end of the seventh year, Jacob said to Laban, "My time is up. Give me my wife."

Laban invited all the men of the settlement to come to a wedding feast. Late that night Laban brought the heavily veiled bride to Jacob. The veil and the darkness kept Jacob from seeing her face.

Next morning Jacob found that Laban had brought him his older daughter Leah instead of Rachel. Seven years of hard work, and now he had the wrong woman! Leah was a gentle person, but Jacob loved Rachel.

Jacob went to Laban and asked angrily, "Why have you done this? I worked for Rachel. Why have you tricked me?"

Laban pretended to be doing the right thing. "In this country it is the custom to give the older daughter first. I thought you knew."

"But I wanted Rachel," Jacob insisted.

"Wait until the marriage festivities for Leah are over," Laban said. "I will give you Rachel too—if you promise to work another seven years."

Jacob had no choice. Because of his great love he agreed to do what Laban asked. At the end of the week he married Rachel.

Leah was an unselfish, steady wife. She bore Jacob sons and a daughter. Rachel bore no children, but he still loved her most. Finally, after seven years, Rachel had a son. She and Jacob named him Joseph.

Now Jacob had been in Haran fourteen years. He longed to see his homeland and his parents. They would be delighted with their grandchildren. Besides that, he was tired of the way Laban kept cheating him.

Soon after Joseph's birth, Jacob said to Laban, "I want to go back to my own country. Let me take my wives and my children."

"Please don't leave," begged Laban. "The Lord has blessed me because of your being here. What more must I pay to get you to stay?"

"I have served you faithfully," Jacob reminded him. "Your flocks and herds have grown. You have become rich. But what about me? When shall I provide for my own family?"

"What shall I give you?" asked Laban.

"Let me go among your flocks today," said Jacob. "Let me take the black sheep, and the cattle and the goats that are speckled and spotted. They are few. Give them to me as wages."

"Good," said Laban. "It shall be as you say."

Laban, however, got to the animals first. He removed most of the black sheep and the speckled, spotted cattle and goats. Then he gave them to his own sons, who took them away.

Jacob relied on God in a vague sort of way. But he had not yet learned to be honest and just toward others when they were not fair with him. So Jacob decided to cheat Laban. He bred large numbers of black sheep, and speckled and spotted goats and cattle. Some of these he traded for camels, asses, servants.

Laban's sons didn't like having Jacob become wealthy. "He has taken what should be ours," they told Laban. "Jacob has made himself rich at your expense."

Laban became less friendly. He kept changing Jacob's wages. But through God's favor, Jacob prospered. Then he had a dream in which God said to him, "Go back to the land of your birth. I will be with you."

Soon after that, Jacob asked Rachel and Leah to come out to the field where he was with his flocks.

"You know how hard I have worked for your father these twenty years," he said. "Yet he has cheated me again and again. But God has not let me be hurt by all of this. Now God has told me to leave this country and go back to the land of my birth. Will you go with me?"

"Our father has given us no share in profits from your

labor," said Rachel. "He even looks upon us as outsiders. Let us leave."

Leah agreed with Rachel.

It seemed best to plan to leave secretly. A short time later, Laban went off to shear sheep. He would be gone for several days. Jacob and his herdsmen got together his share of all the animals.

Servants packed household goods and tents. Children, excited over the move, ran around chattering and asking questions. Jacob had his own questions. What would Laban do when he got back and found Jacob, Leah, Rachel, and their children gone?

Next morning, Jacob set off for Canaan with his wives and children, his servants and herdsmen and their families. He looked forward to being back home. But fear plagued Jacob. How would his brother Esau act toward him?

JACOB'S NEW NAME

After Jacob and his people left Haran, they camped on the side of Mount Gilead. Late in the afternoon Jacob saw a cloud of dust. It seemed to be horsemen approaching at great speed. Then Laban rode out of the dust toward camp.

"What do you mean carrying off my daughters like captives?" he demanded. "Why didn't you let me kiss my grandchildren and say goodbye?"

"I came away secretly because I was afraid you would take your daughters by force," Jacob said.

"I could hurt you," Laban sputtered. "But God spoke to me last night saying, 'Be careful not to speak either good or bad to Jacob.'"

"What is my crime that you have pursued me?" asked Jacob. He went on to remind Laban of all that he had suffered while serving him. "By day heat wore me down. Through cold, sleepless nights I protected the flocks. I spent fourteen years to earn your daughters, six years for the animals. God has seen my struggle and my hard work. That is why He appeared to you last night."

Laban suddenly became more reasonable. "These

women are my daughters, and these children are my grandchildren. How could I harm my own daughters and grandchildren? Come now, let us be at peace."

Jacob got a stone and set it up as a pillar. Then he told his servants to pile up rocks as a landmark.

"This heap stands between us as a witness of our vows," said Laban. "I will not cross this boundary stone to attack you. And you will not cross it to harm me." He called the place Mizpah, or Watchtower.

Laban spent the night at Jacob's camp. Early next morning he kissed his daughters and grandchildren good-bye and gave them his blessing. Then he started for home.

Jacob, his family, and servants broke camp and traveled on toward Canaan. The youngest sons darted in and out of the caravan to explore, pick up colored rocks, or watch gazelles and lizards.

The closer they got to Canaan, the more uneasy Jacob became. How were his parents? Would Esau still be angry with him?

East of Jordan he called men to him to send as messengers to Esau in Edom. He wanted to send a courteous message to his older brother.

"Tell him this," he directed. " 'Your servant Jacob says, I have been living with our uncle until now. I have sent these messengers to tell you I am coming. I now have oxen, sheep, servants. It is my hope that I will find favor in your sight.' "

When the messengers came back they said, "Esau is coming to meet you. Four hundred men are with him."

Jacob was terrified. If Esau had meant to forgive him, would he be bringing a small army with him? He must be planning a battle, Jacob thought. Running away had not solved anything.

Immediately Jacob divided the people and animals into two groups. "If Esau attacks one group, the others can escape," he told his servants.

Afterward, Jacob prayed to God. "I don't deserve all the love You have shown me," he admitted. Then he went on, "Deliver me from the hand of my brother Esau. I am terribly afraid that he will come and kill me and my wives and children. But at Bethel You promised to do me good."

Jacob decided to send a present to Esau. He chose several hundred goats, cows, camels, donkeys, bulls, and sheep. These he planned to send ahead.

Then he told the servants who would be in charge of the first group of animals, "Esau will ask whose servants and animals these are. Tell him they be thy servant Jacob's. The animals are a present sent unto my lord Esau." Then Jacob added, "Perhaps he will then be friendly to us."

That night Jacob was worried and restless. Finally he wakened Rachel, Leah, and his eleven sons. He took them and everything he had across the Jabbok River.

"Stay with the children," he told Rachel and Leah. Then Jacob went back to the campsite.

Jacob was left alone. And then he felt as if a strong man had taken hold of him. All night he wrestled with this "man." Toward morning the "man" said, "Let me go, for the day breaketh."

"I will not let you go until you bless me," Jacob said.

"What is your name?" the other said.

"Jacob."

"Now you will be called Israel instead of Jacob. You will be a prince and have power with God and man."

Receiving such a blessing after the long night spent wrestling was very important to Jacob. He said, "I have seen God face to face, and my life is preserved." And he named the place Peniel because it means "the face of God."

Jacob felt he had more than a new name. As Israel he had a new nature. He had let go of the material way of looking at everything. And he could trust God to guide him instead of trying to get ahead through his own scheming. The one God, the God of Isaac and Abraham, not only had spoken with him again but would be always present.

At sunrise Jacob joined his family. Then in the distance he saw dust swirling up. People were coming toward them. The figure in front could be Esau.

Jacob arranged his family in a column. Then he ran ahead to meet his brother. As he approached he bowed down seven times to show his respect for him as an older brother.

Esau ran forward. Jacob could feel tenderness in the hug Esau gave him. It told him that Esau had forgiven the wrong Jacob had done. Both men cried from relief and joy.

"Who are these people with you?" asked Esau.

Jacob introduced his wives and children.

Then Esau asked, "What were all those flocks and herds I met as I came?"

"They are a present for you."

Esau shook his head. "There is no need for that, my brother. I have enough. Keep what you have."

"Please take them if I have won your favor. Then it will be as if I had found favor with God."

Esau finally took the gift.

After they had talked a long time, Esau said, "Let us break camp and travel on together. My men and I will stay with you and lead the way."

"As you can see," said Jacob, "some of the children are small. The flocks and herds have their young; they shouldn't be driven too hard. You go on ahead. We will follow at a slower pace and meet you later."

"Let me leave some of my men with you," Esau suggested.

"No need," Jacob told him. "It is enough that I enjoy your favor."

Esau started back to his home. Jacob and his household traveled at a slow pace, stopping to camp and rest for fairly long periods as they had done all along the way.

Then God said to Jacob, "Move on to Bethel."

Obedience had become important to Jacob. Now he also wanted his family and servants to serve the one true God. "Get rid of all the idols and strange gods you brought with you," he told them.

They came to Jacob bringing the foreign gods and the rings they wore in their ears. He buried these under an oak tree.

At Bethel, Jacob set up a pillar of stone as before. It was here God had appeared to him on his way to Laban's house. Now God renewed the change of Jacob's name to Israel. Canaan would belong to Jacob-Israel and to his children and their descendants, the Israelites of the Bible.

Jacob had looked forward to having Rachel see his parents and homeland. On the way there, Rachel gave birth to a son, but she lived only a short time after that. When Jacob reached Mamre where his father had his home, he learned that his mother had died. But Isaac was delighted to have Jacob, Leah, and his grandchildren with him. And he was happy that Jacob and Esau were friends again.

When Isaac died, Jacob was ready to take his place as

leader of the tribe. He had found God's way of choosing a leader was the highest. Guided by Him, Jacob took his place with Abraham and Isaac as founders of Israel, a people special to God.

The story is found in Genesis, chapters 25 through 35.

DREAMER, SLAVE, PRISONER

Seventeen-year-old Joseph had a dream. He wanted to talk about it instead of keeping it to himself. "Last night I dreamed . . . ," he said to his older half brothers.

"Not again," taunted Judah.

"Listen," Joseph said. "We were in a field binding sheaves. My sheaf stood up in the field. Your sheaves surrounded it and bowed before it."

"So you think you're going to rule over us?" jeered his brothers.

Later Joseph had another dream. "See here," he said to his brothers and his father, Jacob. "I dreamed that the sun, moon, and eleven stars bowed down before me."

Joseph's ten older brothers scowled and muttered angrily among themselves.

Usually Jacob approved of what Joseph said and did. But now his father scolded him. "What sort of dream is this?" he asked. "Shall we all indeed bow down to you?"

Because of his dreams and his big ideas, Joseph's brothers treated him in rude, mean ways. They also resented their father's favoritism. Joseph had a long coat of many colors that Jacob had made for him. His brothers wore rough shepherd's cloaks. They had to tend the sheep, and this meant battling wolves, weather, and robbers. Joseph often stayed at home.

His brothers were jealous because he had special privileges. What they didn't realize was that Jacob had been devoted to Joseph's mother, Rachel. She had died when Joseph's younger brother, Benjamin, was born. Now Jacob especially favored Joseph and Benjamin.

Besides that, Joseph was a loving, obedient son. Jacob could always trust him to do what was honest and right.

One day, Jacob wanted news of Joseph's older brothers. To get better grass for the sheep, they had gone to a valley near the city of Shechem.

"Go to Shechem," he told Joseph. "See if all is well with the sheep and your brothers. Then bring me word."

"Yes, Father," said Joseph.

He knew this meant about a three-day walk. He got bread and dates, put on his fine coat and set off.

At Shechem, a man told him, "Your brothers have gone on to Dothan." Joseph thanked him and headed north.

Near Dothan, on a green hillside, he saw his brothers. He hurried toward them eagerly. Although they often laughed at him, he still loved them. As he drew closer, he waved and called out.

Instead of giving any sign of welcome, his brothers huddled together. They seemed to be arguing about something. When he got close to them, their faces were sullen.

"Here comes the dreamer," said Levi.

"Why don't we kill him?" asked another one of the brothers.

"We must not kill him," insisted Reuben who was oldest.

Joseph was terrified. Before he could think what to do, his brothers rushed at him. They stripped off his coat. Then they dragged him to a pit and roughly threw him into it.

The pit had no water but it was deep and dark. The walls were too steep and smooth for Joseph to climb out.

Joseph had been hungry and thirsty. Now he was shaken up and bruised. What hurt worst was the thought that his brothers hated him. What did they intend to do to him? Would they leave him in the pit to die?

What Joseph didn't know was that Reuben planned to rescue him later.

Joseph's brothers sat down near the pit to eat lunch. He could hear them talking.

"Look!" he heard Judah say. "A caravan of merchants is coming this way. Let's sell Joseph to them for a slave. Why kill him? After all he is our brother. And it would be better to have the money."

Joseph wanted to come out of the pit alive. But it would be terrible to be a slave. He listened tensely as his brothers haggled over what the traders should pay.

Then a rope was lowered and Joseph was pulled out of the dark pit. At first the sunshine made him blink, then he saw that he was now in a caravan of slaves. The owners were Ishmaelites, sun-tanned desert men—headed for Egypt.

His life had been saved. But for what? He might be sold to a cruel master.

During the days that followed, the caravan moved southward. Hot winds and sun seared Joseph's skin. If his pride had helped build his brothers' hatred against him, it was no part of him now. Without family and friends he

had no hope except in turning to God, as his father had taught him.

After many days, the caravan came to a border city of Egypt. Along its narrow streets were houses and temples unlike any Joseph had ever seen. In a bustling marketplace, drums beat. Flies buzzed and droned. Merchants squatted behind piles of melons, silks, sandals, spices. Joseph could smell perfumes and spices, but also dust and animals.

He and the other slaves were herded to an open space at one end of the market. Buyers with cold, curious eyes prodded him and pinched his flesh or felt his muscles.

After a while, Joseph heard someone shout, "Make way for Potiphar, Captain of Pharaoh's Guard."

The man they called Potiphar came over and looked at Joseph in a kindly way. "You are mine now," he said, and paid the merchants for Joseph.

At first, Joseph was Potiphar's personal servant. But although Potiphar treated him well, no one really cared about what happened to him.

But Joseph knew that no matter where he was, God was with him.

Whether he was in the house or out of it, Joseph began to learn all he could about Egyptian customs and beliefs. He started to learn the language and got along with others.

Joseph became the most willing and best servant he could. Potiphar often congratulated him on his honesty and trustworthiness and gradually he gave him more responsibilities. Joseph even helped with business affairs.

After Joseph had been with Potiphar for several years, his master called him to him. "You are to be overseer over my house. All that I have I put into your hand."

Joseph managed the house well. But then a problem

came up. Potiphar's wife was attracted by his youth, good looks, and pleasing personality. She wanted Joseph to pay attention to her when Potiphar was away.

Time after time she said to Joseph, "Lie with me."

Joseph kept saying no. He respected Potiphar and would not be disloyal to him. "How can I do this great wickedness and sin against God?" he asked her.

One day Potiphar's wife grabbed Joseph's coat and held on to him. He slipped out of the coat and ran off. When Potiphar got home she showed him the coat, and lied, saying Joseph had tried to make love to her.

Potiphar called Joseph to him. "I trusted you all these years," he said, "and now you have done this." So Potiphar had Joseph thrown into prison.

Stunned by what had happened, Joseph lay bound in chains. It had been bad enough to be a slave, but this was much worse. He had tried to do the right thing, and this was his reward!

Instead of complaining, Joseph was patient and meek. The keeper of the prison put him in charge of other prisoners. Among these were Pharaoh's chief butler and his chief baker; they had lost favor with Pharaoh and had been sent to prison.

One morning both these men seemed very unhappy. "Why are you so sad today?" Joseph asked them.

"We have each had puzzling dreams," the butler told him. "In the palace, magicians could help us. But there is no one here to tell us what our dreams mean."

"Do not interpretations belong to God?" asked Joseph. "Tell me what you dreamed. Perhaps God will help me to explain."

"I dreamed," said the butler, "that a vine with three branches rapidly produced grapes. And I squeezed the

juice from them into a cup and gave it to Pharaoh."

"In three days," Joseph told him, "Pharaoh will free you from prison. Once again you will be handing Pharaoh cups as you did before."

"I'll be free?" the butler asked. "Really?"

Joseph nodded. "When you are back in Pharaoh's favor," he said, "remember me. Ask him to let me out of here. I did nothing to deserve being put in jail."

The baker leaned forward expectantly. "Perhaps the ending of my dream will also be happy," he said. "On my head I was carrying three baskets of food. In the top one were all sorts of baked delicacies for Pharaoh. Birds ate them."

Joseph hesitated and then said, "Within three days, you will die. Pharaoh will order this."

Three days later was Pharaoh's birthday. On that day it was customary for him to review the sentences of prisoners. Officials came to free the butler. They took the baker out to be hanged.

Joseph had hoped the butler might speak to Pharaoh about him. Weeks passed. Then months. The butler must have forgotten.

Still Joseph did not become impatient or bitter. He kept on praying and being a useful prisoner. Joseph trusted God's goodness.

FROM PRISON TO PALACE

Joseph had spent two long years in prison. One morning the jailer came to him in great excitement. "You are to get ready to go to Pharaoh," he said.

"To Pharaoh?" Joseph echoed in surprise.

"A messenger came from the palace," the jailer explained. "The palace is in an uproar. Pharaoh has been upset by his dreams. His magicians, wizards, no one can tell him what his dreams mean. The butler suggested sending for you."

The jailer gave Joseph clean clothes and told him to shave. Guards came to take him to the palace. Pharaoh sat in an elevated chair of gold in his audience hall. Magicians, astrologers, wizards, stood around in uncomfortable silence. The stars, the charts, had failed.

Pharaoh said abruptly, "I have had dreams that must be a warning. But no one can interpret them. I have heard it said that you can explain the meaning of dreams."

"It is not in me," said Joseph. "But God can give Pharaoh the answers."

Joseph listened carefully as Pharaoh told his dream. "I was standing on the banks of the river. Seven fat,

51

sleek cows came up out of the water. Then seven skinny, bony cows came up and ate the healthy-looking cows."

Pharaoh paused a minute, looking anxious and distressed. Then he said, "I also dreamed that seven withered ears of corn swallowed up seven plump, full ears."

When he had finished, Pharaoh looked hard at Joseph. But Joseph knew that answers to difficult questions did not come through his own cleverness. He felt that God had sent a message to Pharaoh. And if Joseph listened for guidance he would know what the message was.

"The two dreams have the same meaning," he said in a strong, clear voice. "It's God telling you what will happen. For seven years there will be good crops and plenty in Egypt. These will be followed by seven years of famine."

As Joseph stopped speaking, silence filled the room. Pharaoh and the others knew famine meant withered fields, lack of water, hunger.

Pharaoh frowned. Almost as if speaking to himself he asked, "What must be done?"

"I suggest that you find a wise man to put in charge of the land," said Joseph. "Have him appoint overseers to gather one fifth of the food into royal storehouses during the good years, to save for the time when no food grows."

Pharaoh seemed impressed. He talked to his assistants briefly. Then he turned to Joseph.

"Since God has shown you all this, there is none so wise as you are. You shall be in charge of my palace and my land. Only I will outrank you."

Pharaoh took off his own signet ring and put it on Joseph's finger. He dressed him in fine clothing and then placed the royal golden chain about his neck.

A short while before, Joseph had been a prisoner. Now he was second only to Pharaoh. Joseph had served as well as he could when in prison. Because he had trusted God and followed His direction, he was ready for the work that lay ahead.

Joseph had never lost his loyalty to his own people. But now he also began to feel loyalty to the Egyptians, partly because Pharaoh gave him an Egyptian wife.

To check on food supplies, Joseph went by chariot throughout the land. Only high officials could travel in this way.

"Hail!" people called out as the chariot approached. "Pay heed. Bend the knee!"

But being treated with respect did not change Joseph. He still stopped to talk with slaves and went among the common people.

The biggest crops grew in fields along the Nile. Each summer the river overflowed. When the waters moved off the land, they left black, fertile soil.

"Don't waste anything," Joseph told the farmers. "Overseers will collect a part of all the crops you grow to save for years of famine."

The rules were enforced. At harvest time part of all crops went into newly built granaries.

As he traveled throughout Egypt, Joseph learned about the country. It was ahead of other countries in engineering, art, science. He visited pyramids, statues, awesome temples.

Along the Nile he saw ducks, herons, large white ibises with black heads and tails, and other wildlife.

Joseph liked his work and knew it was important. But he continued to give the credit to God for all the good in his life. When his first child was born, he named him Manasseh: "For God hath made me forget all my toil, and all my father's house." And when his wife, Asenath, had a second son, Joseph named him Ephraim, for, he said, "God has caused me to be fruitful in the land of my affliction."

For seven years, the Egyptians had more food than they could eat. But then a season came when the Nile ran low and was polluted. Crops withered and died. Sheep were wobbly for want of grass and fresh water.

Joseph looked out at the dead, dying earth. Things were bad, but the Egyptians would have been much worse off without the stored grain.

People began saying, "We have no grain to make bread. Our children are hungry."

"Go to Joseph," Pharaoh told them. And Joseph opened the granaries. He began distributing the grain wisely, knowing it had to last for many years.

The famine had spread to other lands. From far countries caravans began coming to Egypt which was like the storehouse of the world.

Joseph wondered if people in his homeland were hungry. "Is there also famine in Canaan?" he asked one group of travelers.

"Even there," they told him.

One day Joseph sat on a platform in a chair of gold and ivory listening to pleas of foreigners who were asking to buy grain. When he saw ten bedraggled, hungry-looking men, Joseph held his breath. They were his brothers! His hands gripped the arms of his chair. "Where are you from?" he asked roughly.

"From the land of Canaan," they told him. "We have come to buy grain."

Pain, sorrow, joy flared up within him. Instantly he remembered his youthful dream about eleven sheaves bowing down to his sheaf.

His brothers looked up with awe and misgiving, but not one of them recognized him. He had been only seventeen when they had thrown him into the pit. Now he was thirty-nine and smooth-shaven. He spoke Egyptian, was called by an Egyptian name, and wore the robes of high office.

Joseph had no wish to punish his brothers for the way they had treated him. But he did need to know whether *they* had changed. Did they still act in hateful, jealous, cruel ways? He also wanted to know whether his father and Benjamin were still alive.

Joseph decided that at first he would not tell them who he was. He would test them. Speaking through an interpreter Joseph acted stern; he made his voice harsh and suspicious.

"You are spies," he accused. "You have come to see the nakedness of the land."

"No, my lord," Reuben protested in a weak, frightened voice.

"We have come to buy food," said Simeon.

"We are all one man's sons," added Judah, as if saying no man would risk so many sons on a spying mission.

"You have come to see the nakedness of the land," Joseph said a second time.

"Your servants are brothers, twelve in all," said Levi. "The youngest is with our father in Canaan. One is not."

So Benjamin and his father were alive! Joseph could hardly wait to tell his brothers who he was. But he wanted first to know what kind of men they had become.

Joseph decided to put his brothers in prison until he had a plan. God would show him what he should do next.

FAMILY UNITED

At the end of three days Joseph had his brothers brought out of prison. "Nine of you are free to leave and take food to your families," he told them. "One of you must stay here in prison. He will be released when you return with your youngest brother."

His brothers started talking among themselves, not knowing that Joseph understood Hebrew.

"This has happened because of what we did to Joseph," said Zebulun.

"Didn't I tell you not to do it?" asked Reuben. "Now we are to suffer because of it."

It sounded to Joseph as if his brothers had changed. But was it only because they were afraid? Joseph left the room, and wept. Then he decided to go ahead with the testing.

Back with his brothers, he chose Simeon as the one to stay. "Now, go," he told the others. "When you come back with your younger brother, Simeon will be freed."

Secretly he told his steward, "Fill their grain sacks with corn. In each sack put back the money they brought to pay for it. Also give them provisions for the journey homeward."

Months went by. Joseph's brothers did not come back. He wondered if his father would let the family starve rather than send Benjamin. And if they were going to let Simeon stay in prison.

Also Joseph didn't know how distressed his brothers had been when they found money in their grain sacks. Nor did he know how hard it was at home to persuade their father to let them take Benjamin and return to Egypt. Only when the family faced starvation again, did Jacob agree to let Benjamin go.

Finally Joseph's brothers did return. They brought back the money they had found in their sacks. They also brought money to pay for the grain they hoped to buy.

Joseph received them briefly, then told his steward, "Bring these men to my home and prepare a feast for them." His brothers suspected a trap and were afraid.

When they got to Joseph's house, the steward greeted his brothers and brought Simeon to them. When Joseph came at noon, his brothers bowed and gave him gifts— perfume, spices, wild honey.

"Our father sent these," Levi told him.

"Your father?" said Joseph. "I hope he is well. Thank him for these gifts." Then he turned to Benjamin. "Is this the youngest brother of whom you spoke?" Again Joseph began crying and had to leave his brothers.

When he returned, Joseph invited his guests to the table; his brothers were surprised when he seated them in order from oldest to youngest. He sat at a table apart but kept sending delicacies over to his guests, especially to Benjamin. As they ate the royal food, his brothers began to relax and enjoy themselves.

When the feast was over, the brothers left to get their grain.

Joseph instructed his steward, "Give them all the grain they can carry and food for the journey. And put my own silver cup in the sack of the youngest."

A short time after his brothers left, Joseph again called his steward. "Follow those men. Say to them, 'Ye have done evil. The silver cup of my master has been stolen.' "

The steward was puzzled. "But you gave it . . ."

"I have changed my mind," said Joseph. He wanted to test his brothers further. He wanted to know what they would do when they found Benjamin was in trouble.

When the steward came back he had Benjamin but the brothers had chosen to return also. They were frightened.

Joseph was pleased that the brothers had stood by Benjamin instead of going off without him. Still he frowned.

Speaking through an interpreter he asked, "What is this you have done? Did you think I would not find you out?"

Judah squared his shoulders and stepped forward. "What shall we say? We are all your servants. Both we, and he in whose sack the cup was found."

"Only the man in whose sack the cup was found shall be my servant," said Joseph. "He alone is guilty."

The brothers were even more troubled and sad. Judah then told how his father had already lost one son. Now he loved Benjamin above the others. Only because his loved ones were starving had Jacob been willing to let Benjamin come.

"When my father sees Benjamin is not among us, he will die," said Judah. "Please let me stay in his place," he begged.

Judah was the one who had suggested selling Joseph. Now he was offering his life to save Benjamin. He and his brothers all seemed worried about their father. This was the exact opposite of the way they had once acted.

Joseph needed no further proof. He turned to his aides, weeping. "Go out, all of you," he said.

Then he turned to his brothers. "I am Joseph," he said.

Joseph's brothers stood trembling. Not one of them could speak.

"Come near to me," Joseph said. "Truly, I *am* Joseph. Do not be angry with yourselves because you sold me. God sent me here to save life. And He has provided for our family in this time of drought and famine. Hurry off with your grain. Then come back with our father and your families, your flocks, and herds. You can live near me in Goshen. There will be five more years of famine. But there is enough for all of you; I will look after you."

Joseph and his brothers began hugging each other, with everyone talking at once.

Meanwhile, Pharaoh heard about Joseph's family. He let Joseph know he was pleased. "Have your brothers take wagons to bring the women and children," he said. "Tell them the good of all Egypt is theirs."

Joseph ordered wagons, bread, meat, grain, everything his brothers could possibly need. As they left for Canaan he watched until he could no longer see them.

The dream about his brothers and father bowing down to him had come true. But this wasn't important. Joseph had overcome any pride or desire for revenge after he was sold into slavery. What was important was that he could now help his family.

As he thought back through the years, Joseph saw that God had been close to him all the time.

Skills to manage a large estate and courage to do right had come from God, preparing Joseph for greater responsibility.

When his family came, Joseph took his father and five of his brothers to Pharaoh. Pharaoh showed great respect for Jacob-Israel and arranged for the family to live in Goshen. They were treated as honored guests of Egypt.

The story is found in Genesis, chapters 37 through 47.

MOSES

Joseph became a hero
when he saved Egypt from famine.
Pharaoh and the Egyptian people welcomed
his brothers, his father Jacob, and their
families when they came to Goshen to live.
Even after Jacob and Joseph were gone,
the Egyptians were friendly to those
Hebrews who remained.

For many generations the Hebrews
worked hard. Their flocks increased.
By the time Moses was born, four hundred
years after Joseph, the Egyptians began
to worry about how the Hebrews had increased
in number.

To make sure the Hebrews wouldn't
cause trouble, Pharaoh forced them to
become slaves. They built cities and
waterways, toiled in Egyptian fields
and dug ditches   all the while being
overworked and shouted at.

The Hebrews needed a leader
who would give them hope and renew their
trust in God. That leader turned out
to be Moses.

65

A RELUCTANT ADVENTURER

The pharaoh became so concerned about how many Hebrews lived in Egypt that he gave an order to the people, "Throw every newborn Hebrew son into the river."

But one of the women was determined to save her son. She hid him for three months. Then she made a tiny ark from bulrushes and waterproofed it with pitch. She put her baby in the ark and laid it among the reeds at the edge of the river.

The baby's sister, Miriam, watched from a distance to see what would happen. While she stood there, a daughter of Pharaoh came down to the river to bathe. She saw the little ark and sent her maid to get it. When the princess looked into the boat, the baby cried.

"This is one of the Hebrew children," the princess said. And Miriam could tell she felt sorry for him.

Miriam ran over to her and asked, "Shall I go and find one of the Hebrew women to nurse him?"

"Yes, do!" the princess said.

Miriam ran to get her mother, who nursed the baby until he was old enough to go to the palace. There he was brought up as the son of the princess. She named him Moses.

As he was growing up in the palace, Moses heard that his fellow Hebrews were often treated badly. One day he went out among his own people and saw an Egyptian beating a Hebrew. His anger flared up against the Egyptian. Moses killed him.

The next day, Moses tried to separate two quarreling Hebrews. "Why do you strike your neighbor?" he asked the one who was in the wrong.

"Who made you a prince and judge over us?" the man asked. "Do you plan to kill me as you killed that Egyptian yesterday?"

Moses knew he was no longer safe in Egypt. He fled to Midian on the Gulf of Aqaba. There a man named Jethro welcomed him into his home. Later Moses married Jethro's daughter Zipporah.

Off tending his father-in-law's flocks, Moses spent many hours alone. Once in a while some traveler would come along and tell about terrible things happening to the Hebrews in Egypt. But no one brought news of Moses' sister Miriam or his brother Aaron.

Whenever grass became scarce near his desert home, Moses took the sheep to a new pasture. One day he was moving them toward Mount Horeb, or Sinai, when he saw a strange thing. One of the dry, brittle thornbushes of the desert was on fire but it did not burn up.

"I must see what is happening," Moses said as he went over to the bush. Then he heard a voice calling, "Moses, Moses!"

Moses had learned to listen to God, so now he said, "Here I am," and heard a response.

"I am the God of your fathers, the God of Abraham,

Isaac, and Jacob." This was holy ground! Moses covered his face because he was afraid.

"I have seen the affliction of my people which are in Egypt," said the Lord. "I have come to deliver them and bring them into a good land, a land flowing with milk and honey. I will send you to Pharaoh, so you may bring forth my people, the children of Israel, out of Egypt."

"Who am I that I should go to Pharaoh?" Moses asked. He had been educated in Egypt. But now he was only a shepherd with no special talent. What God wanted him to do called for wisdom, boldness, courage.

"Certainly I will be with you," God promised.

But Moses couldn't imagine the people listening to him. "Suppose I tell them that God has sent me," said Moses. "They will ask, 'What is his name?' Then what shall I say?"

"Say, 'I AM has sent me.' Say, 'The God of Abraham, the God of Isaac, and the God of Jacob has sent me.' Go and gather the elders of Israel together. They will listen. Then you and the elders must go to the king of Egypt. Say to him, 'Let us go, we beseech thee, three days' journey into the wilderness to sacrifice to our God.' "

"The people won't believe me," Moses protested. "They won't do what I tell them to do. They'll say, 'God never spoke to you.' "

Then God told Moses to cast down his shepherd's rod. He threw it on the ground, and it became a serpent. Moses ran from it.

And the Lord said, "Put forth your hand, and take it by the tail." Moses reached out fearfully. But as soon as he caught the serpent it became a rod again. Then God gave Moses a second sign that he could show to the Hebrews as well as the Egyptian magicians.

"Put your hand inside your robe," the Lord told Moses. Moses obeyed. When he took his hand out, it had turned leprous as snow.

Then the Lord again said, "Put your hand into your robe." This time when Moses took his hand out it was clean like the other.

But Moses still didn't see why God had chosen him. Nor did he understand that his ability to do the work would come from God. "O, my Lord, I am not eloquent," he said. "I am slow of speech."

"I will be with your mouth," God told him. "I will teach you what to say and do."

"O Lord, please send someone else," begged Moses.

"Is not Aaron your brother?" the Lord asked. "He can speak well. You can tell him what to say. Even now he is on his way to meet you."

Moses' loyalty had been tested when he stood up for the Hebrew slave in Egypt and when he stopped the quarrel between two Hebrews. Perhaps he could find courage to lead the people. And hadn't God said He would be with him? Moses got the sheep together and started for home.

He went to Jethro, who had always treated him like a son. Moses said, "With your permission, I will go back to Egypt and visit my relatives."

"Go in peace," Jethro told him.

Moses left for Egypt with Zipporah and their sons. On the way they met Moses' brother Aaron. As they traveled north and west across the desert to Egypt, Moses told Aaron what God expected of them.

Back in Egypt, Moses and Aaron called the elders of the Hebrew people together, and Aaron described what had happened to Moses at the burning bush. "You are no longer to be slaves," he said.

71

Moses showed them the signs God had said to use. The elders responded with gratitude and hope.

"But *will* Pharaoh let us go?" one of them asked anxiously. Moses and Aaron went to Pharaoh's palace to get the answer.

"We bring you a message from the God of Israel," said Aaron. "He says, 'Let my people go. They must hold a feast for me in the wilderness.' "

"Who is this Lord that I should listen to him?" sneered Pharaoh. "I will not let the Israelites go."

"Let us go, we pray," said Aaron. "If we don't obey God, plagues or even death may strike us."

Pharaoh was a proud, stern man. He became very angry. "You are taking people away from their jobs," he accused them. "Get back to your work."

That same day Pharaoh sent out orders that the Israelites, as the Hebrews were also called, should work harder. Brickmakers needed straw to bind the mud into bricks. Pharaoh had been furnishing the straw. Now he made the people go to the fields to cut it.

Finding and cutting the straw took time. The slaves couldn't turn out as many bricks as before, and Pharaoh wanted the same number. Their foremen were beaten because of the shortage.

Losing all hope, they came to Moses and Aaron. "May God judge you for giving the Egyptians an excuse to kill us," they said.

Moses was discouraged. God had told him that Pharaoh would at first refuse to let the Israelites leave. This would show his wickedness. In the end, however, the Egyptians as well as the Israelites would see God's power. But right now Moses saw only failure.

When he again prayed to God, Moses asked, "How can

you treat your people like this? Why did you send me here?"

"Tell the people, 'I will make you free,'" the Lord said to Moses. "'I will bring you into the land I promised to give to Abraham, Isaac, and Jacob.'"

Moses told the people what God had said. They were too tired out by hard work, too worn down by whips and curses of their overseers to listen.

Moses and Aaron went back to Pharaoh, as God had told them to do. But he was just as surly and unreasonable as before.

Then plagues began coming upon the Egyptians. First the Nile River turned red. Water in wells and ponds became unfit to drink.

Some time later, slimy frogs invaded the land. They even went into the houses. The frogs were followed by lice, and by buzzing masses of flies. A disease struck cattle, sheep, horses.

Egyptians had experienced all these plagues before, but they had never been so severe. Each time one of the afflictions got really bad, Pharaoh would send for Moses and Aaron. He would say something like, "Plead with your God to take the plague away. And I will let your people go to worship your God."

Each time when the trouble ended, Pharaoh, unwilling to lose workers, would fail to keep his promise. Meanwhile Egyptian men and animals were afflicted with boils. Huge hailstones slammed down. Big clouds of locusts chewed up every growing thing. Famine threatened. Then darkness covered the land for three days, except in places where the Hebrews lived.

Moses was learning more and more that God was all power. Even when the people doubted, he continued to trust. Then the Lord told him, "The time will come when Pharaoh will *ask* you to go."

Moses' confidence that the Israelites would escape from Egypt inspired others. One day he told the people, "There will be one more plague. After that Pharaoh will let you go. Prepare for a long journey. Ask your neighbors to give you jewels, gold, and silver."

Moses knew that some of the Egyptians would help out because they felt sorry for the Hebrews and respected them. Others wanted to win the favor of the God of the Israelites. And Moses himself had become great in the sight of Pharaoh's servants and his people. As part of his own planning, Moses had already sent Zipporah and his two sons back to Midian to stay with Jethro.

The Hebrews listened in silence as Moses told them about a new observance. It was to be called the Lord's Passover and would come on the fourteenth day of the month. This would mark the beginning of the Hebrew year and of spring. That night the Egyptians would lose their oldest sons.

"When that happens," said Moses, "you must be ready to leave Egypt. Eat this last meal in this country with haste."

The meal was to include roast lamb and unleavened bread. This bread would be made with flour, water, and salt. Flat cakes of it would be baked on hot stones. The people were also to eat bitter herbs.

At midnight on the fourteenth day, the oldest son of every Egyptian family died. From the houses came sounds of weeping. Pharaoh, grief-stricken by the loss of his own son, summoned Moses and Aaron.

"Leave us," he said. "Go serve the Lord, you and the children of Israel. Also take your flocks and your herds."

Then he added humbly, "Give me a blessing as you go."

Moses and Aaron hurried back to the waiting Hebrews. There they found Egyptians begging them to leave right away. They were giving them food, clothing, rings, bracelets, animals, gold, silver. The slaves were suddenly rich!

"We are to leave immediately," Moses told those nearest to him.

As the word was passed along, mothers picked up their babies. Men prodded donkeys loaded with pots, jugs, food, tents, tools, blankets. Family by family, tribe by tribe, they moved forward. The earth shook with hundreds of hurrying feet. The journey to the Promised Land had begun. God was delivering His people.

WANDERERS
IN THE WILDERNESS

After Moses and his followers escaped from Egypt they made their way to Succoth. Then they went on to Etham at the edge of the wilderness. There the Lord told Moses to have the Israelites camp by the Sea of Reeds.

The people were setting up camp when a cry went out, "Look! Pharaoh has sent his army after us!"

Great numbers of Egyptian chariots rolled rapidly toward the camp. The Israelites had no weapons. They rushed around in a panic.

Some, forgetting all Moses had done for them, came up to him and cried, "Have you brought us out here to die in the wilderness? Why did you make us leave Egypt? Didn't we tell you to let us alone?"

"Don't be afraid," Moses told the people. "The Egyptians you are looking at—you will never see again. The Lord shall fight for you."

Then the Lord said to Moses, "Wherefore criest thou unto me? Speak unto the children of Israel that they go forward. Hold your rod over the water. Stretch out your hand over the sea and divide it. The children of Israel shall go on dry ground through the midst of the sea."

Moses walked calmly down to the seashore. Meanwhile a pillar of cloud settled in front of the Egyptians and kept them from advancing. Moses stretched his rod over the sea. A mighty east wind began pushing the water back until there was dry land between two walls of water. The people stared, hardly daring to believe what they saw. Moses stepped forward. "Come," he said.

Through the night, the Israelites crossed safely to the opposite shore. Next morning the Egyptians started to follow, but their chariots bogged down in the marsh.

The Lord said to Moses, "Stretch out your hand over the sea."

When Moses did this, the waters covered the chariots, horsemen, and Pharaoh's army.

"We are safe! We are free!" the people shouted. They moved on, singing as they went.

That night the people talked excitedly around their campfires. Moses was admired for his deeds and abilities. But he knew he had not done it alone. In Egypt, Moses had learned to listen and then to do what God commanded. People had turned to him for answers. Moses knew he was ready for whatever lay ahead.

To show their gratitude for protection and guidance, Moses and the children of Israel sang together, "I will sing unto the Lord: The horse and rider he hath thrown into the sea; the Lord is my strength; He is become my salvation."

But songs were forgotten when Moses and his followers reached the wilderness of Sin. People found the empty spaces and silence frightening. They didn't like scorpions, spiders, snakes, the mournful cries of jackals.

As the Israelites traveled across the hot sands, dust settled on their clothing. The flocks and herds could only move slowly. The Promised Land seemed far away.

Then Moses' followers began having trouble finding food. People remembered Egyptian cucumbers, fish, melons. Everyone began to grumble. "It would have been better to die in Egypt," said some. "There we had plenty to eat."

To Moses and Aaron they complained, "You have brought us into this wilderness to kill us with hunger."

Moses went off by himself to pray. "Tell the Israelites they shall have meat to eat," the Lord said to Moses. "And in the morning they will have plenty of bread. Then the children of Israel will know that I am the Lord, their God."

That evening great flocks of quail flapped over the camp. They flew so low and so heavily that the Israelites could catch them with their hands. Next morning small, round, white things covered the ground. They looked like a kind of frost.

"What is it?" the people asked.

"It is bread that the Lord has given you," Moses told them. "Gather what you need for today, but do not keep any overnight."

Some feared that this would be the last of what they called manna, so they gathered more than they needed. But by morning it had spoiled.

After that, manna appeared every day except on the sabbath. On the sixth day of the week, people could gather a two-day supply which would not spoil. Women roasted the manna, boiled it, ground it. But after a while the people grumbled about its sameness.

Moses had many different responsibilities in addition to finding food and water. The Israelites wanted to be free people, but they didn't know how to govern themselves or make decisions. They expected Moses to be their judge, leader, prophet, priest, lawyer.

People came whining to him about a missing black lamb or dislike for a neighbor. What bothered him most was that the people seemed to worship God only halfheartedly. Some had even brought idols with them. Moses knew the people should worship the one true God.

The Israelites traveled on across the Sinai desert. Three months after they left Egypt they came to Midian. It was at Mount Sinai, sometimes called Horeb, that Moses had seen the burning bush and God had told him to bring the people there. The mountain was steep and almost bare. But grass, palms, and tamarisk grew in well-watered oases around it. Moses told the people to camp for a while. Here they would learn more about God.

One day Moses' father-in-law, Jethro, came to the camp. He noticed that people kept coming to Moses.

"Why are they standing in line all day to see you?" Jethro asked.

"They come to me with their disputes," Moses explained. "I am their judge. And I teach them God's rules and laws."

"It is not good," Jethro exclaimed. "You are wearing yourself out. This is too big a burden for you."

"What can I do?" asked Moses.

"Divide the people into groups of thousands, hundreds, fifties, and tens, with a leader for each group," Jethro told him. "Let the leaders take care of small problems. This would leave you free to deal with important matters."

Moses saw this could be a good way of organizing the people, so he followed Jethro's advice. He took great care in appointing judges and leaders. Then he got to thinking about the need for laws to keep the people united, orderly, obedient. Abraham and other leaders had given the people some rules. Moses had added instructions telling the people how to act in many situations. But the Israelites needed to have laws that came directly from God, not a person.

One day the Lord called Moses to the top of Mount Sinai. There, over a period of forty days, God gave Moses a very special set of laws. These laws, later known as the Ten Commandments, were more just, more wise than anything Moses could have thought of. They would show the Israelites the need to put God first in their lives.

The first commandment was, "Thou shalt have no other gods before me." It was followed by three commandments, showing the people's duty to God.

Then came the call to honor one's father and mother. The final commandments, showing the people's duty to each other, told them they were not to kill, commit adultery, steal, bear false witness, or covet what was not theirs. If the people obeyed these rules, they would be able to think rightly and act rightly.

As Moses was going down the mountain to take the laws to the people, Joshua came up to meet him. He was chief of one of the twelve tribes of Israel and often helped Moses.

Together they went on. As they got close to the camp, Joshua and Moses heard loud singing. Then they saw a golden calf before an altar. People were dancing and singing around it. How could they be worshiping an idol at the very time Moses had been getting laws from God? Had they so quickly forgotten how God had cared for them? They didn't act as if they had learned anything about God or the need to trust and obey Him.

Moses hurled the stone tablets on which the laws were carved to the ground and broke them. As he strode into camp the merrymaking stopped. People looked up ashamed and afraid. Moses walked over to the altar and seized the golden calf. He burned it and ground it to powder.

Then he turned on Aaron, whom he had left in charge. "What made you do this?"

"Don't be angry," Aaron pleaded. "You know how the people are. You were away so long they thought you weren't coming back. They wanted gods to go before them. The people gave me pieces of gold. I cast them into the fire, and this calf came out."

Moses was furious because the people were stubborn and unruly. But when most of them seemed sorry about making the golden calf, he prayed for their forgiveness.

Later the Lord said to Moses, "Cut two tablets of stone. I will write upon them the same commands that were on the tablets you broke."

Always trusting, always obedient, Moses cut out the stone. Once again he climbed Mount Sinai.

END OF A JOURNEY

The second time Moses climbed Mount Sinai to get the Commandments from God he spent another forty days during which he neither ate nor drank. When he came down from the mountain, his face shone. And this time he found the people had been faithful.

Once more Moses told the people about the laws they were to obey. But now they also needed a place in which to worship. He asked for materials with which to build a tent of meeting. "It is God's will that we do this," he said.

The Israelites, grateful that God had forgiven their disobedience, brought gold, silver, linens that the Egyptians had given them. These were used to make and adorn the sacred chest, called the ark, and also the tent, table, lampstand, and altar.

When it was finished, the tent of meeting had two rooms with a curtained court. In the inner room was the ark. It was made of acacia wood and overlaid with gold. Inside the ark lay two stone tablets with the Commandments on them.

Moses hoped that the tent of meeting, or tabernacle, as it was also called, and the ark would be continual reminders of God's presence. In the tent he listened to God. There he received directions and encouragement to pass along to the people. If he and the people would only listen, trust, and do what was right, they would have what they needed, and they would get to the Promised Land.

Moses and his followers stayed at Sinai about a year. When they left, the ark went with them. The chest had rings at each corner. When poles were passed through these, it could be carried from place to place.

Every time the Israelites set up camp, the tent of meeting was pitched in the center. When a cloud covered the tent, they stayed in the place where they were. If the cloud lifted, they journeyed on.

In times of hardship and danger, the Israelites again forgot what God had done for them. "You must trust God," Moses would tell them. But sometimes the people weren't willing to listen to him; they turned bitter or resentful.

At one point even Moses' sister, Miriam, sided with his critics. She became jealous because of the Ethiopian woman he had married. Also, Moses was always giving the people a message from God. Wasn't Miriam herself a prophetess? She and Aaron decided they should have more honors for themselves. "Hasn't the Lord spoken through us too?" they asked.

But Moses was able to forgive those who opposed him. When Miriam got leprosy, he prayed for her healing. For seven days she was shut out of the camp, but when she was healed, he was glad to have her travel on with the Israelites.

Finally, Moses and his followers reached Kadesh in the wilderness of Paran, where they found an oasis and plenty of water. Moses hoped that his mission might soon be over. Instead of rushing ahead, he waited for directions.

"Send men to search the land of Canaan," God told him. "One man from each tribe."

Moses chose twelve tribal leaders. "See what the land is like," he told them. "Also what the people are like. And whether the land is fertile or poor. See whether the people live in tents or fortified cities. Be of good courage, and bring back some of the fruit of the land."

Many days later, the scouts came back. Two of them carried a huge bunch of grapes on a pole between them.

"What did you see?" asked the people as they crowded around and eyed the grapes.

"There is plenty of water, good fields of grain," said one of the scouts. "We saw pomegranates, figs, honey."

"But the people living there are powerful," said another scout. He sounded tired and scared. "Their cities are well fortified."

One of the scouts, named Caleb, had seen the same sights as the others. But he was a man of action and faith. "Let us go up and possess Canaan," he said. "We are well able to conquer it."

"They are too strong for us," one of the scouts contradicted. "We felt like grasshoppers beside these men. They are as tall as giants."

The Israelites had walked and walked to get to the place where they were. God had parted the waters of the sea for them. Manna had fallen. Water had been produced in unusual ways. Moses himself knew that trust in God could make possible things that looked impossible. But the people didn't dare to claim the good that was there.

To go in and take the land looked too dangerous to

some of them. Sad and discouraged, the Israelites went back to their tents.

That night, the people complained about Moses and Aaron—even about God. They cried out, "We wish we had died in Egypt."

"Let us choose a leader and go back there," they said one to another.

This appealed to some troublemakers, who had forgotten how miserable they had been as slaves. They went from tent to tent stirring up the people. Then these hotheads went to Moses and Aaron.

Caleb and Joshua came forward and tried to reason with the people. "Don't rebel against the Lord," said Caleb.

Angered by Caleb's words, someone cried out, "Stone them."

But just then a glow appeared over the tabernacle. The people saw this as a sign of God's protection of Moses. Silently they went away. But the people had rebelled against God, who had led and provided for them so faithfully. They had lacked trust. Before they could enter the Promised Land they had to learn to obey God and to love God.

After he had prayed, Moses called the people together. "Caleb and Joshua will enter Canaan, which God promised our forefathers," he told them. "But not one of you over twenty who has complained against God will go into the land. You and your children will have to wander in the wilderness forty years."

The sorrowful people turned back into the wilderness. Season followed season. New hardships, new setbacks, came to the Hebrews. They had battles with fierce desert tribes.

At Kadesh everything seemed to go wrong. One day when there was no water to drink, rebellious men came to Moses and Aaron. "Why did you bring us here to die?" they shouted. "Here there is no place for seeds or figs or vines. There isn't even water to drink."

Moses and Aaron didn't argue. They went to the tabernacle to pray. "Call the people together," God told Moses. "Take the rod and speak unto the rock. It shall give forth water."

Moses and Aaron had the people come to a big rock at the edge of the camp. Then Moses struck the rock twice. Water gushed forth. There was plenty for the people and their flocks and herds.

As the Israelites wandered year after year, Moses taught the people to listen to God, to love and to serve Him. By the end of forty years Moses was leading a whole new generation. Children of the slaves who came out of Egypt had been born free. They had become strong through obeying the laws God had given Moses. It was time to choose a new leader to guide the Israelites into the Promised Land.

"Get Joshua," God told him.

Moses called the Israelites together and said, "I will not go over the river Jordan with you. But God will go before you. And Joshua will be at your head."

To Joshua and the others Moses said, "Be strong and of good courage. The Lord will not fail or forsake you."

When Moses knew the time had come for him to leave, he again called the people together. Then he and Joshua taught them a song God had given them: "Ascribe ye greatness unto our God. He is the Rock, his work is perfect . . . just and right is he." The song reminded the Israelites of times when they had been disobedient. Yet

God had kept them as an eagle that fluttereth over her young.

At the end of the song Moses said, "You must think about these laws and pass them on to your children. These laws are not mere words. They are as close to you as your life." Through these laws the children of Israel would be able to govern themselves once they got to the Promised Land.

The Israelites stood silent and serious as Moses blessed them tribe by tribe, saying "The eternal God is thy refuge, and underneath are the everlasting arms . . . Israel then shall dwell in safety alone . . . Happy art thou, O Israel."

The people began to weep. They knew Moses' work had ended. He had brought their parents, crushed by slavery, out of Egypt. Through his selflessness and love he had won their confidence and inspired them. Because he had listened to God and trusted, Moses had been able to give the Israelites God's Commandments to live by.

All would be well with Israel. All was well with Moses. He had no fear about the future of his people. That he would not enter the Promised Land with them did not matter. He had already entered it in thought.

The story is found in Exodus, chapters 2 through 20; Numbers, chapters 10, 12 through 20; and Deuteronomy, chapters 5, 31, 32, and 34.

5

JOSHUA

A PROMISE KEPT

Joshua had been chosen to go on with the work that Moses began. He had told the people that God had promised this land to them. Now a big task lay ahead of Joshua. How could he lead the Israelites into Canaan?

Joshua and the Israelites had a camp at Shittim in the hills not far from Canaan. They would have to cross the Jordan River, then face the Canaanites, who had strong fortifications.

Whenever tempted by doubt or fear, Joshua turned to God. As he prayed he heard the message, "Arise, go over Jordan. As I was with Moses, so I will be with you. Be strong and courageous."

Joshua sent officers among the thousands of Israelites and others to tell them to get food ready for the march. Then he talked to leaders of the tribes who had settled in the hills east of the Jordan River.

"Let your wives, children, and cattle stay here," said Joshua. "But your armed men must go with us to conquer Canaan. After the conquest you may come back here."

"All you command, we shall do," the leaders replied. "We will obey you as we obeyed Moses."

Joshua needed to know about Canaanite strengths and weaknesses. He chose two spies. "Go scout the land on the other side of the Jordan River," he told them. "Especially the city of Jericho."

The men came back before long. During the first day in Jericho they had pretended to be travelers. They had taken lodging for the night with a woman named Rahab. Her house was built in the city wall.

"The king of Jericho heard we were spies and sent men to seize us," one of the scouts told Joshua. "But Rahab hid us on the roof under stalks of flax. Later she lowered us to safety through a window facing fields beyond the outer wall. We hid three days as she told us to."

"We promised Rahab to return her kindness," said the other man. "When we take Jericho, we are to see that she and her family are safe."

"How about fortifications?" asked Joshua.

"Strong," one of the spies admitted. "Jericho has two walls around it. And the people seem well armed."

"But Rahab told us that they fear us," said the other spy. "They have heard about what God has done for the Israelites. Rahab says no courage is left in any man. The Lord has put the land into our hands."

Next morning Joshua had the people break camp. "We will march to the Jordan," he told them.

The people set off along a hard path down into the valley. When they reached the banks of the river, they were dismayed. In a dry season they could have forded easily. Now the Jordan, swollen by rain and melting snow from the highlands, was wide. There was no bridge. And the Israelites had no rafts.

After three days of waiting, a crossing still seemed impossible. But Joshua dared to trust God. "Tomorrow," he

told the people, "the Lord will do wonders among you."

Next morning the river looked the same. But Joshua asked the people to get ready to cross. When the ark reached the Jordan, the waters would pile up and leave a path, he said. The people began taking down tents.

Joshua sent the priests ahead. They carried the Ark with the Ten Commandments, the symbol of God's presence. As soon as the feet of the priests touched the Jordan, the water far upstream piled up in a heap. Downstream the water ran on into the salt sea. A great dry place was left.

Men, women, children, flocks, herds crossed safely. "At last! The Promised Land!" people cried out as they marched forward happily.

That night the people camped at a place called Gilgal, only a short distance from Jericho.

Joshua had asked one man from each tribe to bring a stone from the riverbed. Now he had the men pile them up as a monument. Then he spoke to the people, "In the future your children will ask what these stones mean. Tell them how the Lord our God dried up the Jordan and kept it dry while Israel crossed."

In memory of the night their parents and grandparents had escaped from Egypt, the Israelites celebrated the Passover. The next day they gathered grain and fruit from the land. The people no longer needed the manna which had fed them in the wilderness. None fell.

One day Joshua walked close to Jericho to see how it might be captured. The citizens, afraid of what the Israelites might do next, had closed the massive gates. To Joshua the walls seemed high and forbidding.

When Joshua lifted up his eyes, he had a vision. He saw a man with a sword in his hand. Joshua went over to him. "Are you with us or with our enemies?" he asked.

"As captain of the army of the Lord have I come," he answered. "Take off your shoes, for you stand on holy ground."

Then the Lord gave Joshua a plan for the capture of Jericho. It was a very unusual battle plan. But Joshua had asked for help; he was ready to do anything his God commanded.

Back at Gilgal, Joshua called the priests together to explain the plan. "Each day for six days we will march around Jericho," he told them. "A group of armed men will lead. Seven priests blowing trumpets of rams' horns will follow. Behind them will come priests bearing the ark. They will be followed by a rear guard and the people. On the seventh day, Jericho will fall."

On the first day of marching, Joshua warned, "Do not let your voices be heard."

Each day for six days Joshua's followers marched once around Jericho. The ground shook under their feet. Dust rose. The horns blasted. Weapons clanked. But no one spoke a word. After their strange march, the Israelites went back to camp.

The people of Jericho were baffled and terrified. They couldn't understand such behavior. No Israelite shot an arrow. No one tried to batter down gates or scale the walls.

On the seventh day, Joshua told his men, "God has already given us Jericho. Today you will walk around the city seven times instead of once. When the priests blow the rams' horns loud, all of you must shout with all your might."

As they had before, the people marched silently. On the seventh time round, the priests blew shrill blasts on their trumpets of rams' horns.

Then Joshua yelled, "Shout! The Lord has given you the city." The people shouted all together while the horns sounded. And the wall fell down flat.

Joshua remembered how Rahab had saved his spies. "Bring out Rahab and her family," he said. "Take them to your camp where they will be safe."

The Israelites took the silver and gold and bronze and iron for the Lord's treasury. Then they burned the city and everything in it.

They had captured Jericho. But Canaan was made up of a number of small city states. Each was ruled by a king. These had to be overcome one by one.

Most of the time, Joshua and his men had very little trouble taking a city. But once some Gibeonites tricked him. They came to Joshua at Gilgal.

"We have traveled from a distant land to ask for a peace treaty," they said.

The men wore ragged clothing and patched sandals.

"Who are you?" asked Joshua. "Where do you come from?"

"We are from a distant country," one of them insisted. "We have heard of the might of your God. We are your servants. Therefore, make peace with us."

To prove that they had come a long way, they showed Joshua their dry, moldy bread. "And see how worn our clothing has become from the trip," said one of them.

Joshua believed them. Ordinarily he would have prayed before doing anything as important as making a treaty. This time he yielded to their friendliness and their praise of him.

Three days later, Joshua found out the strangers were Gibeonites from four neighboring cities. They lived in places the Israelites had intended to take. Because he had made a treaty with them, Joshua would not attack. He did summon their leaders.

They admitted they had lied to save their towns from attack. "But now we are in your hands," they said. "Do with us as you wish."

Joshua ordered the Gibeonites to become woodchoppers and water carriers for the Israelites.

Over a number of years the Israelites had taken much of Canaan.

"Divide the land among the tribes," the Lord told Joshua. Joshua obeyed. For a time there were problems between the tribes, jealousies and disagreements about boundaries. But gradually peace came to the land; a tribal league was formed.

Joshua reminded the people that God had kept His promise of a land flowing with milk and honey. They should put away any worship of other gods and renew their trust in the Lord. God had brought the people to the Promised Land. It was up to them to keep it a land of promise.

The story is found in Joshua, chapters 1 through 13, 23, and 24.

RUTH

Before Israel had kings,
the people were governed by judges.
Usually the judges were more like tribal
heroes than officials who decided on rights
and laws. The Bible tells us of twelve judges over
a period of about two hundred years.

Many of the Hebrews turned to
other gods during this period, and people
were often suspicious of outsiders.
The story of Ruth took place while the judges
were leading the Israelites, perhaps sixty
years before David, her great-grandson,
was born.

LOYAL RUTH

Ruth grew up in the country called Moab, east of the Dead Sea. Often she met strangers who had left their homelands because of famine. The Moabites almost always had food enough to spare.

Among the strangers were two brothers—Mahlon and Chilion. They had come with their parents, who were Israelites, from Bethlehem. Ruth and Mahlon became friends, and later they were married.

Ruth, who was warmhearted and unselfish, trusted and loved her mother-in-law. She accepted the one true God that Naomi worshiped, even though her own people had worshiped nature and many strange gods.

Many years passed happily. Then Mahlon and Chilion both died.

"Now I am without husband or sons," Naomi said to Ruth and Orpah, Chilion's widow. "I will return to Bethlehem."

The three women set off together. They had gone only a little way when Naomi said, "It would be better for you to go back to your parents' homes. May the Lord treat you as kindly as you have treated me and my sons. And

107

may He bless each of you with another happy marriage."

Naomi kissed Ruth and Orpah goodbye, and they began to weep.

"No," they said. "We will return with you to your people."

"Why should you go with me?" Naomi asked. "I have no more sons for you to marry."

Orpah and Ruth understood Naomi's longing to return to her own country. She owned land there and would be among friends and relatives. But it might be difficult for them to live in a land with strange customs and to leave the people they loved.

It was a hard decision. The three women wept again. Then Orpah decided she would go back to her own people. She kissed Naomi, then slowly turned away, her duty done.

But Ruth had no intention of leaving Naomi.

Naomi pleaded with her, "Your sister-in-law has gone back to her own people, her own gods. It would be best for you to do the same."

"Please don't ask me to leave you," Ruth said. "Where you go, I will go. Where you live, I will live. Your people will be my people. Your God will be my God."

When Naomi saw that she could not convince Ruth to go back, she said no more. The two of them went on together. They passed fields of waving grain and pastures where sheep cropped grass. They descended into the stark Jordan valley, made their way north of the Dead Sea, crossed the Jordan River and climbed the mountains of Judea. Finally they came to Bethlehem.

In this small town everyone knew everyone else. As soon as they arrived, people began talking about the two women.

"Is it really Naomi?" one of the women asked another.

At that moment Naomi felt sorry for herself. She forgot the good years with her husband and sons, the loyalty of Ruth.

"Don't call me Naomi," she told her old friends. "Call me Mara." "Mara" means bitter. "I went out with a husband and two sons. I have come home empty."

Ruth and Naomi had shelter, but they needed food. Fortunately the barley harvest was just beginning. Men with small sickles went into the fields to cut the grain. These reapers were followed by men who bound the stalks of grain into sheaves.

Reapers and binders always left some stalks on purpose. And they did not harvest the part of the crop growing in the corners of the fields. The poor, the fatherless, and the widows were allowed to go into the fields and gather this free grain. This was called gleaning.

Ruth knew some owners weren't as kind to strangers as others. And some gleaners might not welcome foreigners. But she was willing to try.

"Let me now go to the field and glean ears of grain," Ruth said to Naomi.

"It would be a good thing," Naomi told her. "Go, my daughter."

Ruth got up very early the next morning. Not far outside Bethlehem she saw big fields of barley. Some men were sharpening the hand sickles, or short curved knives. Others were already reaping and binding. Would the owner of the fields let her share his barley?

Ruth summoned her courage and walked toward the overseer. "I pray you let me gather and glean," she said.

"Over there." The overseer pointed to where women were picking up stalks one by one.

To get the stalks Ruth had to bend, bend, bend. Dust swirled in her face. The sun beat down mercilessly. Picking up the stalks made her hands sore. Sometimes other gleaners pushed in ahead of her. Reapers shouted at them if they followed too closely.

Occasionally reapers and gleaners rested in the shade or stopped to get a drink of water. Ruth worked steadily, resting only once.

After a while, the master came to the field. "The Lord be with you," he greeted the laborers.

"The Lord bless you," they called back.

"Who is that man?" Ruth asked the woman gleaning closest to her. She wasn't sure she would get an answer. Until now the other gleaners had paid little attention to her.

"His name is Boaz," said the woman. "He owns the field."

"Listen, my daughter," he said, coming over to Ruth. "Do not go to glean in another field. Keep close by my maidens." His voice was gentle. "When you are thirsty, go and help yourself to the water the young men have drawn."

"How can you be so kind to me?" asked Ruth. "I am only a foreigner."

"Yes, I know," said Boaz. "I also know about the love and kindness you have shown your mother-in-law. How you left your father and mother and your own land. May a full reward be given to you by the God of Israel you have come to trust."

"Thank you, sir," said Ruth. "You have given me comfort."

Ruth went back to work. At lunchtime, Boaz called, "Come and eat with us."

Boaz gave her more bread and parched barley than she

could eat. That afternoon she found barley by the handful instead of by the stalk. Boaz had told the reapers to let Ruth glean among the sheaves. He had also told them to leave many heads of grain unharvested.

At the end of the day, Ruth knocked off the heads of grain to take them home. She had a bushel.

When Ruth got home, Naomi looked at the grain and exclaimed, "So much! Praise the Lord for whoever was so kind to you."

"The name of the man for whom I worked is Boaz," said Ruth.

"Boaz?" Naomi sounded excited. "He is a close relative of my husband's."

"He told me to come back," said Ruth.

"This is a good thing. Do as he says," Naomi advised.

Morning after morning Ruth went back to work in the barley fields with the maidens of Boaz. After the barley harvest was finished, she gleaned in the wheat fields of Boaz. Nights she talked to Naomi about her work, the other gleaners, and about Boaz.

After the harvest ended, Naomi said to Ruth, "Shall I seek a home for you, that it may be well with you? Boaz has been kind to you and he is a relative."

Ruth listened while Naomi told her exactly how to prepare to see Boaz. "Bathe," said Naomi. "Use perfume, and put on your best clothes. Then go to the threshing floor of Boaz. Let him finish eating and drinking. Then speak to him. He will know what to do."

As usual, Boaz showed respect and understanding. He again praised Ruth for her kindness to Naomi, and he accepted her fully even though she was from Moab.

"You are a woman of worth," Boaz said. "I wish to buy Naomi's land so that I can marry you. There is only one problem. Another man is a nearer kinsman and has the first claim to the land. And he could have you as his wife if he wished."

That very day Boaz talked with Naomi's relative. The kinsman gave Boaz the right to buy the land. Now Boaz was also free to marry Ruth.

A short time later, Ruth and Boaz were married. Naomi lived with them. She was delighted when Ruth had a son named Obed, and she took care of him.

Neighbors came to admire the child. To Naomi they said, "He is the son of your daughter-in-law, who has been kinder to you than seven sons. May his name be famous in Israel."

Ruth's love for Naomi had kept her with her mother-in-law, even when it meant going to a strange new land. In the end her kindness was returned. She had a good home, friends, a husband who cherished her.

And Ruth's son became important. For Obed became the father of Jesse, and Jesse was the father of David, a famous king of Israel.

The story is found in the book of Ruth.

7

SAMUEL

Joshua led the Israelites into Canaan
and divided the land among the tribes.
But after he died, the people faced many problems.
The lay of the land, some of it hilly or gashed
by ravines, some below sea level, made it
difficult for the people to unite.
Also, the Hebrews had been herdsmen.
It seemed hard to settle down and be farmers.

For many years the same thing happened
over and over again. The Israelites would disobey
the Commandments and worship the
gods of their neighbors. Trouble
would come—usually oppression
by their enemies.

Then the people, forgetting their
neglect of Him, would pray to the Lord.
A tribal leader who was called a judge
would arise to help the people defeat their
invaders and win peace. These judges also tried
to show the people the importance of obeying God.

Of the twelve or more judges who led
the Israelites, Deborah and Gideon
are among the best known.

But the greatest of all the judges
was Samuel. Unlike most of the others,
he was not a military leader. He went on
circuit among three towns settling disputes.
Samuel was also a priest and God-appointed
prophet. He represented God as a leader
of the people and in choosing and
counseling their kings.

PROPHET AND KINGMAKER

Samuel grew up in a temple of the Lord. For many years his mother, Hannah, had longed for a son. She prayed to God, "If you will remember me and give me a son, I will give him in service to the Lord."

Hannah's prayer was answered. She named her boy Samuel because, she said, "I have asked him of the Lord." When he was three years old, Hannah took him to the temple at Shiloh. There he lived with the high priest, Eli, who was a gentle, kind person. He treated Samuel like a son and taught him priestly duties.

Once a year, Hannah and her husband Elkanah came to the temple to offer a sacrifice. They told Samuel about his younger brothers and sisters at home. Hannah always brought a little coat she had made for him.

Several years passed. One night, just after Samuel had gone to sleep, a voice called, "Samuel."

"Here I am," Samuel answered and ran to Eli.

"I didn't call you," said Eli. "Go and lie down."

The same thing happened two more times. After the third call, Eli said, "It must be the Lord speaking to you.

If the call comes again, say, 'Speak, Lord. Your servant hears.' "

Once again Samuel heard his name. This time he answered, "Speak, for your servant is listening."

Then the Lord told Samuel that because of the evil ways of his sons, Eli's family would be destroyed. In the morning Samuel was afraid to tell Eli what he had heard. But Eli insisted, and after Samuel gave him the terrible message, the old priest said, "It is the Lord; let Him do what seems good to Him."

The people had already begun to think of Samuel as a prophet, a person who listened to God and was a spokesman for Him.

One day bad news came to Eli and Samuel. In a battle with the Philistines, the Israelites had been defeated. Eli's two sons, Hophni and Phinchas, were killed.

His sons had been disobedient; still Eli loved them. When he heard they were dead and the ark of God had been captured, Eli died.

The Philistines were delighted to have the ark; they took it to Ashdod. There they placed it in the temple of one of their gods, Dagon, who they believed was half-man, half-fish.

Twice the idol Dagon fell over on its face before the ark. The second time its head was cut off. Then sickness came to the people of Ashdod.

Being superstitious, the Philistines thought the ark itself was causing trouble. Seven months after seizing it, they put the ark into a cart along with golden offerings. Then they hitched two cows to the cart and set it, without a driver, on the road to Beth-shemesh. When the Israelites in Beth-shemesh saw the ark, they rejoiced.

But the ark itself had no power or magic. What was

needed was for people to obey the Commandments that were on tablets inside the ark. Samuel told the people, "Put away strange gods. Serve the Lord only, and he will deliver you out of the hand of the Philistines."

The Israelites did get rid of their idols and images. But they were still afraid of the Philistines. Samuel sent out word for the people to meet at Mizpeh, a few miles from Jerusalem.

On the day agreed upon, people left their pots, plows, shops, and homes to come to Mizpeh. There the Israelites fasted. "We have sinned against the Lord," they confessed. They begged Samuel to pray to God for them.

Samuel was offering a sacrifice when a messenger came. He called out breathlessly, "The Philistines are marching toward Mizpeh."

The people were very frightened. While Samuel continued praying, the Philistines drew closer and closer. Then suddenly there was a terrible sound and shaking like thunder where the Philistines were. Their horses bolted. Foot soldiers broke ranks. The Israelites chased the Philistines to their homeland and won back the cities that had been captured.

After that, people turned to Samuel as their judge and prophet, the only head of their government. Year after year he held court in Bethel, Gilgal, Mizpeh. Samuel looked to God for answers and had courage to set right what was wrong.

When he grew older, Samuel appointed his sons Joel and Abiah as judges. Joel and Abiah were dishonest. They decided cases in favor of whoever paid them the most money. The people didn't like them.

One day the elders of Israel came to Samuel. "Your sons do not walk in your ways," one of them said.

Another interrupted, "Give us a king to judge us like all the other nations."

Samuel was upset. He had led the people in the way he believed would please God. Now they wanted a king.

He asked for time to pray. God told him, "Listen to the people. They have not rejected thee, but they have rejected me. Hearken unto their voice. But warn them what it will be like to have a king."

When he returned to talk to the elders, Samuel warned, "A king will take your sons for his chariots and to be his horsemen, to serve in his army. Some of your sons will have to reap his harvest, make instruments of war. A king will take your daughters to be cooks. He will take your fields, vineyards, and sheep. You will be his servants. You will cry out because of your king."

The elders refused to listen. "We will have a king over us that we may be like all the nations," they insisted. "A king may judge us, go out before us, fight our battles."

Samuel saw it was useless to argue. When he prayed, the Lord told him, "Hearken unto their voice."

Then Samuel said to the elders, "You shall have your king. Now each of you go to your own city."

Later the Lord told Samuel, "Tomorrow about this time I will send a man out of the land of Benjamin. You will anoint him to be captain over my people."

The next day as he was leaving his city, Ramah, to go to the high place to make a sacrifice, Samuel saw a tall, handsome stranger entering the city. "This is the man who will rule my people," the Lord said to Samuel.

The young man, Saul, had come to ask Samuel if he could see in a vision where he might find some lost donkeys that belonged to his father, Kish.

"The donkeys have already been found," said Samuel.

"Come eat with me, and tomorrow I will send you on your way."

The next morning, when Saul and Samuel were alone at the end of town, Samuel took out a vial of oil. Then he said to Saul, "The Lord has appointed you to be king of Israel."

It was the custom to anoint with oil the head of a person chosen for high office. In his conversation with Saul the night before, Samuel had hinted that this would happen. Now Saul was awed and silent as Samuel poured the oil on his head.

Some time later, after Saul had united the tribes, he was officially crowned as king of Israel. But people still turned to Samuel as their religious leader.

During the early months of Saul's reign, Samuel was pleased. Courageous and bold, Saul went from one success to another. He won victories against the Philistines and other people who were attacking the Israelites. But then Saul became ruthless in his fighting and turned away from God. After Saul had been king for several years, the word of the Lord came to Samuel saying, "I am sorry I have set Saul to be king; for he is turned back from following me."

Samuel went to Saul and said, "You have rejected the word of the Lord. Now he has rejected you from being king of Israel."

Samuel turned away. Saul grabbed at his robe to try to hold him back. The robe tore.

"See?" said Samuel. "The Lord has torn the kingdom of Israel from you."

Even after he returned home, Samuel grieved for Saul. Samuel understood that it had been hard for Saul to stand up for what God wanted. But perhaps Samuel had failed to show Saul that he must always obey God.

Then one day the Lord said to Samuel, "How long will you grieve over Saul? Go to Bethlehem and find a man named Jesse. I have provided me a king from among his sons."

"How can I go?" asked Samuel. "If Saul hears of it, he will kill me."

"I will show you what to do," the Lord told him.

Samuel went to Jesse's house in Bethlehem. "I am come peaceably to sacrifice to the Lord," he said. "Call your sons to the sacrifice."

As Jesse's sons came in, the prophet thought the tall, good-looking Eliab must surely be God's choice. But he prayed silently to be sure.

"Look not on his countenance or on his height," the Lord said. "I have refused him. Man looks on the outward appearance, but the Lord looks on the heart."

One by one, Jesse had seven of his sons pass in front of Samuel.

"Are these all of your sons?" asked Samuel.

"Well, there is the youngest," said Jesse. "But he is out tending the sheep."

"Send for him at once," said Samuel.

David soon came running. He was a fine-looking boy with clear eyes and a ruddy face. He looked strong and brave.

The Lord said to Samuel, "Arise. Anoint him."

After anointing David, Samuel went back to Ramah. Still people came from all over to ask his advice.

Samuel did not live to see it, but he knew David would be a great king. And he was able to help David when Saul turned against him.

When Samuel died, all of Israel honored him. People

remembered that he had chosen a king for them. As a judge he had helped settle disputes and guarded sacred laws. But most of all people remembered that Samuel had always trusted God and acted with courage.

The story is found in I Samuel, chapters 1 through 16.

DAVID

SHEPHERD, HARPIST, WARRIOR

Day after day, David tended his father's flocks on the hills near Bethlehem. Always he listened and watched. He listened to the hum of insects, the calls of birds. And he listened to God.

To make himself ready to protect his flock, he practiced hurling stones with a slingshot. Several times when a bear or lion attacked the flock, David saved the lambs. He could be brave, because he knew God was caring for him.

Tending sheep was often a lonely job. To help pass the time, David played a small harp. He also made up songs.

One time when he was tending sheep, David was called home by the prophet Samuel, who anointed David's head with oil and told him that someday he would take Saul's place as king of Israel.

Another day when David was in the fields, an older brother came running and said, "You are to come at once."

At home, David found messengers from Saul. "An evil spirit troubles the king," one of them said. "Music might soothe him. He has commanded us to find a good musician."

Because the king had sent for him, David had no choice except to obey. He took his harp and went to Gibeah, where Saul lived.

David's music did help Saul. It calmed him when he became restless or gloomy, or burst into a rage. Saul soon made David his armor-bearer and personal attendant, a position of trust and honor.

A short time later Philistines invaded the land. Saul and his army camped in the valley of Elah and grouped themselves for the battle. But threats from a Philistine giant named Goliath terrified the Israelites.

Young David had trust in God, not in weapons or brute strength. Armed only with his slingshot, he ran toward the giant and killed him.

After that, David served in Saul's army. He was so brave and efficient that Saul made him a captain. At first, Saul was pleased with David's successes.

But one day when David returned from battle, women crowded around him singing and dancing. They sang "Saul hath slain his thousands, and David his ten thousands."

Saul was extremely jealous and no longer wanted David as his personal attendant. At times his jealousy put him in a rage.

David had a steady and close friend in Jonathan, Saul's son. "We will be as brothers," they had promised each other. Jonathan gave David his robe, his sword, and his bow as tokens of their friendship. And Jonathan told his father, Saul, how loyal David was, and how the Lord favored him.

Saul pretended to be pleased with David and promised

that he could marry his daughter Michal if David won a big victory over the Philistines.

Despite Saul's hopes, David came out of every battle unhurt and undefeated. The people loved him more and more.

Saul's jealousy turned to hate. The way things were going, David might be the next king instead of his son Jonathan. Now at times Saul acted like a madman.

One day Saul asked for music. David had played only a few chords on his harp when suddenly, Saul rose from his seat and threw a spear at him. David leaped up and ran to safety.

Later, David was at home with Michal. They had just been married. Saul sent guards to surround the house.

Michal loved David and she was very upset. "If you don't get away tonight, you will be killed tomorrow," she said.

Michal fixed up a dummy and put it in David's bed. If soldiers came around during the night, they would think he was still there. Then she let David down by a rope from a window.

David got away without rousing any of the guards. He didn't worry about Michal because he knew Saul wouldn't do anything to his own daughter. But what should *he* do?

Samuel might help. David made his way through the night to Ramah, where Samuel lived. The prophet gave him food and listened to what he had to say. Samuel still believed that David would be king someday. David decided to try to talk to his friend Jonathan secretly.

"What have I done? What am I guilty of that your father seeks my life?" David asked Jonathan when he found him.

"I am sure my father has no thought of *that!*" said

Jonathan. "He would have told me. But what do you want me to do?"

"I will hide in the field until the day after tomorrow," said David. "Meanwhile find out how your father feels about me."

David and Jonathan agreed to meet in the field on the third day. "You stay behind those stones," Jonathan told David. "I will shoot three arrows as though I shot at a mark. If I tell my servant, 'The arrows are on this side of you,' it means you can come out and return with me. If I say to him, 'The arrows are beyond you,' it means it is not safe for you; Saul intends to kill you."

The two men vowed to remain friends, no matter what happened.

In three days Jonathan returned to the field and shot an arrow. He said to the lad with him, "The arrow is beyond you." Then Jonathan sent the lad back to the city so he could meet secretly with David. They wept together and finally Jonathan said, "Go in peace. The Lord be between you and me forever."

David escaped from Saul. But at first he had no food, shelter, or weapons. David set up quarters in a cave in a limestone area near Adullum. Some of his relatives and a number of men, angered by Saul's arrogance and his treatment of David, joined him there.

Saul treated David like an outlaw and sent his army after him. At times, Saul himself led his soldiers. David and his men could never stay long in one place.

David prayed to know where he should go and what he should do. He found safe places where he and his six hundred men could hide. These men loved David because of his fairness and generosity.

One day when David was in the hills of Ziph, Jonathan came to his camp. "Don't be afraid," Jonathan told him. "I found you, but my father will not."

He and David talked about their future. "You are noble and strong," said Jonathan. "You will be king of Israel. I will be next to you."

Before Jonathan left, he and David renewed promises of everlasting friendship.

Some time later, David and his followers were resting in a large cave in the wilderness of Engedi near the Dead Sea. From the back of the cave, David heard muffled voices and commands at the entrance. Then he saw a familiar figure. Saul! Because of the depth of the cave, the king did not see David and the others.

"This is your chance," one of his men whispered to David. "He is in your power."

David had suffered because of Saul. But this did not give him the right to kill his king. Besides that, David remembered when Saul had been almost like a father to him.

He inched forward in the dark and with his sword cut off a piece of the bottom of Saul's robe. But then he whispered to his men, "I should not have done this. It is a sin to injure God's chosen king."

These words kept David's men from killing Saul, who soon left the cave. David followed him at a distance. Then suddenly he called out, "My Lord the king."

Saul looked around startled.

"Why do you listen to people who say I want to hurt you?" asked David. "Back there in the cave you were in my power, but I spared you." David held up the piece of cloth he had cut from Saul's robe. "Just look," he said. "I cut off a piece of your robe. But I didn't kill you. Doesn't

134

this show that I am not trying to harm you? I have not sinned against you."

Saul began to weep. At that moment he saw himself honestly.

"You are a better man than I am," he called out. "May the Lord reward you for your kindness. I know now you are surely going to be king. Swear to me you will not kill my family."

"I promise," David told him. But Saul still pursued David.

Near Carmel, David and his men were so positioned that they acted like a protective wall around the thousands of sheep belonging to Nabal, a man of wealth. No marauders made off with his flocks while David was there.

Sheepshearing time came. Nabal would be giving a feast. David felt his men had a right to share in it, so he sent messengers asking for food.

They came back empty-handed. "He was mean-tempered," said one.

"He asked us, 'Who is this David?' " added another. "He told us his food was for his shearers, not for a gang of men he didn't even know."

"So it was no use that we protected this man's territory," David said angrily. "If he won't give us food, he'll be sorry. Buckle on your swords."

On the way to Nabal's place, David and his men met a number of people coming toward them. They drove asses loaded with huge quantities of food. A woman was riding with them. When she saw David, she dismounted, then bowed before him.

"Please listen to me," she said. "Nabal is a fool. But don't pay attention to what he said. I have brought presents."

The woman explained that she was Nabal's wife, Abigail. She had been shocked when Nabal refused to help David. Without telling her husband what she was doing, she had ordered servants to get food ready for David and his men.

"Even when you are chased by those who seek your life, you are safe in the care of the Lord," Abigail told David. "After you have become king of Israel, you won't want the causeless shedding of blood on your conscience."

"Bless you for your good advice," said David. "We accept your gifts. Go in peace."

That night, David and his men feasted on bread, roast lamb, parched corn, raisins, and fig cakes. David was grateful for the food. He was even more grateful that he had been kept from killing Nabal and his people. God was indeed caring for him.

A KINGDOM WON AND LOST

David, his followers, and their families fled to Gath, a Philistine city. There King Achish offered them a town called Ziklag, in the southern part of Philistine territory. In return for a place to have their camp, David and his men were to defend the area.

At Ziklag, David ruled as a desert chieftain. He also trained his men. Through raids he added to his little domain. His men also protected neighboring Judah, where David had been born and his own tribe lived. He made friends among the leaders there.

One day David and his men returned from helping Achish and found their camp had been burned to the ground.

David's men had always given him their love and loyalty. But now, tired and grieving, they threatened to turn against him. David was distressed and uncertain what to do. His two wives, Abigail, whom he had married after Nabal died, and Ahinoam, had also been taken captive.

David turned to God. "Pursue," the Lord told him. "You will overtake them and recover all."

Then David persuaded his men to go with him to find their families who had been taken captive.

137

They recovered their wives and children, all unharmed. They even got back their stolen property.

Shortly after this, a messenger came running into David's camp. "I have escaped from Saul's army on Mount Gilboa," he panted.

"How did the battle go?" David asked anxiously.

"Our entire army fled," the messenger told him. "The Philistines have won a tremendous victory. Saul and his son Jonathan are dead."

Then David and his men mourned and wept for their king and for the people of Israel, defeated in battle.

David cried out in sorrow for Saul and Jonathan, "The beauty of Israel is slain upon thy high places: how are the mighty fallen!" Mourning for his brave and loyal friend, he sang, "I am distressed for thee, my brother Jonathan . . . thy love to me was wonderful."

As his grief lessened, David wondered if the time had come for him to be king, as Samuel had said he would be. He prayed to know where he should go and what he should do.

"Go to Hebron," God told him. Hebron was in Judah, about twenty miles from Jerusalem.

David's wives, his men, and their families went there with him. Very soon the leaders of Judah came to him. "We want you to be our king," they said.

David was ready. His leadership had already been tested. And he knew God was the source of his strength.

Although accepted in his own tribe of Judah, David still had to win over the northern tribes of Israel. He did not try to force the people there to accept him. He waited and prayed.

After seven years, the elders came to David. "Even when Saul was our king, you were our real leader," they

said. "The Lord said you should be our king." Thus David became king of all the tribes of Israel at last.

One of his first acts as king of the united Judah and Israel was to capture Jerusalem with the help of the men who had been with him in exile. Well fortified, Jerusalem stood on a hill near the borders of both Judah and Israel. It became the capital city, known by the special name of "the city of David."

David had always loved and trusted God. Now he saw the importance of religion to the Israelites; Jerusalem ought to be the religious as well as the national center. To the people, the ark containing the tablets of stone with the Ten Commandments had become the most sacred religious object. David had it brought to Jerusalem.

As years passed, David opened up trade routes. Through defeating the Philistines, Edomites, and other peoples, he added territory. The nation prospered. People took pride in it. Men who tilled the fields, worked in brick kilns, or served in the army loved and honored David.

David already had several wives, as was the custom. But he fell in love with a very beautiful woman named Bathsheba. Her husband, Uriah, was a soldier. David arranged to have him placed in the front line of the hottest battle. After Uriah was killed, David married Bathsheba.

Nathan, a prophet who came and went at David's court, confronted David with what he had done. He reminded David of all the good that had come from God. "Why, then," Nathan said, "have you despised the laws of God and done this terrible deed?"

David knew he had done wrong, and he was truly sorry. "I have sinned against the Lord," he confessed. As in the psalm he prayed, "Have mercy on me, O God . . . cleanse me . . . create in me a clean heart."

David's favored son was handsome, high-spirited Absalom. As a young adult, Absalom was headstrong, eager for power. He plotted the overthrow of his father. He told the people that David had a weak, corrupt government.

"I wish I were the judge," Absalom would say persuasively. "I would give justice."

Joab, David's commander-in-chief, tried to warn him that Absalom was scheming against him. David was unwilling to listen. Finally, Absalom went to Hebron. There he proclaimed himself the new king of Israel.

A messenger came to David in the palace. "All Israel has joined in a conspiracy against you," he said. "Rebels plan to take Jerusalem."

News of Absalom's treachery hurt David. But to make a stand against his own son seemed unthinkable. And it might mean that Jerusalem would be destroyed.

"We must flee at once," David told his family and followers. Although terrified, his servants stood by David. "We are ready to do whatever you decide," they said.

Then David and his family, his courtiers and servants, and the army itself went out of Jerusalem.

At the brook of Kidron, David talked to Zadok, a priest. He and other Levites had brought the ark out of Jerusalem and planned on following David.

But David decided the ark of God ought to go back to the city. "If I find favor in the eyes of the Lord, He will bring me to Jerusalem again. But if I have displeased Him, let Him do to me what seems good to Him," he said.

He sent the priests with the ark back to stay in the city. But they were to keep in touch with him.

DAVID'S GREATEST GIFT

David's sadness over Absalom's rebellion was eased by the loyalty of his friends. Weeping crowds lined the roads outside Jerusalem.

But some people were not willing to stand by David in bad times. A few onlookers, glad to see him in disgrace, jeered.

At one point, Shimei, who had a fierce loyalty to Saul's family, threw stones at David and shouted, "Get out of here, you murderer."

David's men wanted to lay hands on Shimei. But David wasn't interested in revenge.

"Let Shimei alone," he said. "If my own son seeks my life, what is it to me that this Benjamite curses me. Maybe the Lord will notice my suffering and bless me instead."

Many had risen against him, yet David found comfort. "Thou, O Lord, art a shield for me," he sang.

David and his followers set up a base camp at Mahanaim. Sympathizers brought in food, cooking pots, mats to sleep on. "Your people are hungry, thirsty, and weary," one of them said to David.

Day after day they brought cheese, flour, beans, honey,

and fruit to the refugees. These people remembered the best about David. They wanted him back as king.

From Jerusalem, friends sent messages about what was going on. Some who had favored Absalom lost enthusiasm for him when he turned out to be weak and incompetent. "Go against Absalom," David's backers urged.

David didn't want to fight. But the country was being split apart. His followers bitterly opposed those of Absalom. Finally, David saw he had to take action.

First, David found out how many men were on his side. Then he divided them into three fighting forces, headed by Joab, Abishai, and Ittai.

The day came for the troops to go off to fight Absalom's army. They marched out of the city by hundreds and by thousands. David buckled on his sword. "No, no!" the people cried out. "You shall not go!"

"You are worth ten thousand of us," said one.

"Whatever you think best," said David. Then he told Joab, Abishai, and Ittai, "For my sake, deal gently with Absalom."

David waited at the gate of the city all day, while the battle raged in the wood of Ephraim. At last a man came running. As he neared the gate he cried out, "All is well. The rebels who dare to stand against you are destroyed!"

But David had only one thought. "Is Absalom safe?" he asked.

"I saw fighting, but I don't know," the man answered.

Then a second messenger came running. "I have good news. The rebels have been defeated."

"But is Absalom safe?" David demanded.

"May all your enemies be as that young man is," the messenger answered.

Overcome by grief for his son who had been killed,

David wept and cried out, "O my son Absalom! my son. Would God I had died for you, O Absalom, my son!"

Because of David's sadness, the army's victory turned into mourning. The people went back to their homes almost ashamed of their part in the battle.

But Joab, the commander, protested bitterly to David. "It looks as if you love your enemies and hate your friends. If you don't come out and thank the men who fought for you, who saved you and your family, no one will stay in your service."

David then went out to the gate. The people came to him, and he thanked them for their loyalty.

Surrounded by loyal followers, David set off for Jerusalem. At the Jordan River a great crowd of shouting people had come to welcome him. Among them was Shimei, who had cursed David at the time of his retreat from Jerusalem. Shimei fell down before him and begged, "Please forgive me and forget the terrible thing I did."

"Shall not Shimei die?" asked Abishai.

"Don't talk to me like that," said David. He wanted unity and peace. And today was a day for celebrating his return as king of Israel. David turned to Shimei. "You shall not die," he promised.

There were other battles as David tried to bring all the tribes together and repel outside invaders. But little by little peace came to Israel. Grateful for having been delivered from his enemies, David sang praise to God. "As for God, His way is perfect: the Word of the Lord is tried: He is a buckler to all those that trust in Him."

Years passed and David's son Adonijah began taking steps to have himself made the ruler of Israel. He boasted to his friends, "One day I will be king." But Nathan the prophet and Bathsheba both felt her son Solomon ought to be king, even though he was younger than Adonijah. Nathan suggested that Bathsheba go to David to tell him Adonijah was talking and acting as if he would become king.

"You promised that Solomon, our son, would be king," Bathsheba said to David. "All of Israel is waiting for you to tell them if he is the one you have chosen."

While she was talking, Nathan came in to see David. Bathsheba left. Nathan bowed low and asked, "My master, have you appointed Adonijah to be the next king? He and his followers are right now feasting. Shouts are going up, 'Long live King Adonijah.' "

"Call Bathsheba back," David ordered.

When she stood before him, he said, "I swear unto you by the Lord God of Israel that Solomon your son will reign after me, and he shall sit upon my throne in my stead."

Then David spoke to Nathan, "Solomon is at Gihon. Get Zadok, the priest, and a bodyguard, and go there. Have Zadok anoint Solomon. Take my own mule for my son to ride upon."

As they returned from Gihon to the palace, David could hear trumpets and shouts of "Long live King Solomon!"

David spoke to Solomon about the need to rely on the Lord. "Solomon, my son, serve Him with a perfect heart and with a willing mind: for the Lord searcheth all hearts, and understandeth all the imaginations of the thoughts."

David also told Solomon how he had dreamed of building a great temple to honor God. "But God said unto me, 'Thou shalt not build a house for my name because thou hast been a man of war.' " David wanted Solomon to carry out his plans for a temple.

The leaders of Israel were willing to give gold, silver,

bronze, and precious stones for such a temple. The people gave also. David was pleased. "Now, our God, we thank you. It is in your hand to make great, and give strength to all. May your people always want to obey. And give my son Solomon a good heart."

David's trust in God had grown; Israel had prospered. David would leave a strong, united, and peaceful nation for his son Solomon to rule.

David left another gift too—many songs of praise for God and His care. These continue to inspire people and remind them of the shepherd boy who became a king.

This story is found in I Samuel, chapters 16 through 27, 30; II Samuel, chapters 1, 11, 12, 15 through 19, 22; II Kings, 1, 2.

SOLOMON

TOO MANY WISHES

David had reigned over Israel forty years. When Solomon took over the throne, the kingdom was united and peaceful. The new king wanted to live up to his father's last words to him: "Be strong. Behave like a man. Obey the laws of God." But he had questions. He wondered how he could govern, judge, plan, build, keep the peace, and win the love of the Israelites.

One day, Solomon went to a hilltop altar at Gibeon. There he offered burnt offerings. That night he had a dream in which God said, "Ask what I shall give you."

"I am as a little child," said Solomon. "Give me an understanding heart that I may govern your people. Help me to know the difference between what is right and what is wrong. Who by himself is able to govern your great people?"

"Because you asked for wisdom rather than riches or long life, I will give you a wise and understanding heart," said the Lord. "I will also give you what you have not asked for—riches, honor, and long life."

Even after Solomon woke up, the dream stayed with

him. Later, in Jerusalem, he found the promises coming true.

Solomon very much needed wisdom the day two women came before him with a dispute. One had a baby in her arms.

"Sir," the first woman said. "We live in the same house. Each of us had a baby. This woman's baby died during the night. She then stole my son from me while I slept and laid her dead child in my arms. When I woke up, I saw it was not my son."

"It was her son who died," the other woman interrupted. "This living child is mine!"

"That's a lie!" the first woman said in an angry voice.

The two women argued back and forth. Solomon didn't know which one to believe. But he trusted God's guidance. An idea came to him. Solomon nodded to a servant. "Bring me a sword," he said.

When the servant came with the sword, Solomon commanded, "Divide the child in two and give half to each of these women."

One of the women began to tremble. "No!" she cried out. "Give this woman the child. Don't kill him."

But the other woman said, "Divide it."

"Give the baby to the one who wants it to live," said Solomon. "She is his mother."

When they heard how he had judged who the real mother was, people said, "God has given Solomon great wisdom."

Hiram, king of Tyre, had always been a great admirer of David, and he offered congratulations and good wishes to Solomon.

Then Solomon began to think about the temple the Lord had told David his son should build. Since Hiram seemed friendly, Solomon thought he might be willing to help.

Solomon sent a message to the king. "I am planning to build a house for the Lord. Please help me. Send workmen to the mountains of Lebanon to cut timbers for me. I will send my men to work beside them. And I will pay you whatever you ask."

Happy to be at peace with Israel and to get their wheat and olive oil, King Hiram sent a message to Solomon saying, "I can supply both cedar and cypress. My men will bring the logs from the mountains to the sea and build them into rafts. We will float them along the coast to wherever you need them."

To help Hiram's workers, Solomon sent ten thousand men a month. They would stay in Lebanon a month and then be back home for two months.

In Israel, thousands of workmen cut, dug, hauled, and finished stone. Still others toiled under mountains to bring out copper.

Solomon sent for talented craftsmen to chisel, carve, and do metalwork. Among them was an architect and builder named Hiram, who came from Tyre. He made objects from bronze and adorned great pillars with lilies and pomegranates. Weavers and dyers made fine fabrics of purple, blue, crimson.

It took seven years to finish the temple. But time and money meant nothing to Solomon. The splendid stone temple was to be the most beautiful building in Israel.

The inner walls were of fragrant red cedar and other special woods, richly carved, and overlaid with gold. Lampstands, candlesticks, incense holders glittered with gold. Throughout the temple there were carved cherubim, palm trees, and flowers.

For the dedication of the temple, thousands of people, from shepherds and fishermen to elders and heads of tribes, came to Jerusalem. The sound of song, trumpet, and lyre echoed through the city as people sang and gave thanks. They feasted for seven days.

On the day of dedication, elders and priests carried the ark with the Ten Commandments into the temple. As the priests came out from the inner sanctuary a cloud filled the temple. The cloud was so bright that the priests had to leave.

Then Solomon, magnificent in his embroidered robe, spoke to the crowd. In a long prayer he gave thanks to God for divine protection, guidance, and goodness. "Even the skies and the highest heaven cannot contain You, much less the temple I have built," prayed Solomon. He asked rewards for those who did what was right, forgiveness for those sorry for their mistakes.

At the end of the prayer, Solomon turned away from the altar to bless the people. "O my people, may you live good and perfect lives before the Lord," he said. "May you always obey His laws."

The temple had whetted Solomon's appetite for extravagance. He had a palace built for himself, even more magnificent than the temple. It included many buildings, some of them for the hundreds and hundreds of wives he had. The palace was surrounded by pools, vineyards, orchards, and gardens full of flowers.

At his palace, Solomon dressed in rich clothing. Every meal was a banquet served on gold plates. Nights he slept on a gold bed.

In the hall of judgment, Solomon sat on an ivory throne overlaid with gold. On either side of it stood the gigantic figure of a lion.

To pay for the things he wanted, Solomon began a regular system of taxation. Because farmers paid taxes with part of their crops, he needed storehouses. He also needed stables for forty thousand spirited horses and housing for the drivers of his many chariots. Towns grew up around these warehouses and stables.

Solomon opened up mines, built smelters. He also had a navy. In these boats, Solomon shipped copper, iron, metal objects to African countries. Boats returned with gold, silver, silks, spices, jewels, ivory, peacocks, and apes. Many trade routes crossed Solomon's kingdom. Caravans had to pay tolls.

Luxurious living claimed much of Solomon's attention. But he had once chosen wisdom ahead of riches, and this often showed through in what he did. To keep the country strong, he strengthened the wall around Jerusalem and added fortifications. But Solomon sought peace, not war. Trade treaties helped to keep foreigners friendly. People lived in safety. If they wanted to, men could tend their fields or sit under their own fig tree and write poetry without fear of an enemy swooping down on them.

Solomon was a good organizer. To rule the country, he divided it into twelve districts. Then he appointed talented men to help him. As a judge he was as shrewd and fair as he had been in the case of the two women and one baby.

Scribes wrote down some of Solomon's sayings along with others collected from the past. These came to be known as the book of Proverbs.

Some of the sayings have to do with lessons to be learned from nature. "There are . . . things which are little upon the earth, but they are exceeding wise: the ants are a people not strong, yet they prepare their meat in the summer . . . The spider taketh hold with her hands, and is in kings' palaces."

Other sayings tell about the ways of people. "He that is slow to anger is better than the mighty."

Sometimes Solomon's wisdom took the form of warnings to his people. He stressed obedience to God. "Trust in the Lord with all thine heart," he said, "and lean not unto thine own understanding."

Honor came to Solomon, though his own people did not love him as they had loved David. But they were awed and impressed. "King Solomon has been blessed with great wisdom," they said among themselves.

Throughout the ancient world, sailors, farmers, camel drivers talked about Solomon. "He is wiser than any man who ever lived," they said.

People came from all around to see Solomon's court and get his advice. One of his famous visitors was the queen of Sheba, who lived on the Arabian peninsula over a thousand miles from Solomon's court.

She came partly because Solomon's ships were competing with her camel caravans for trade. But the shrewd, curious queen also wanted to have a look at his wealth. And she came to test his wisdom.

Solomon gave her a royal welcome. Drums and trumpets sounded when she entered the hall of judgment. Solomon showed her the palace, served her choice foods. When she asked hard questions, Solomon answered all of them.

Finally the queen exclaimed, "Everything I have heard about you is true! Your wisdom is greater than I had ever imagined. Blessed be the Lord your God. How He must love Israel to give them a king like you!"

Her visit ended with a kind of treaty. Before she left, the

queen of Sheba gave Solomon gold, great quantities of spices, and jewels. He gave her elaborate gifts—anything she wanted.

To keep up the palace and to satisfy his selfish desire for things, Solomon demanded a great deal of his people. He took the best of their grapes, figs, and grain in taxes. Men of northern Israel had to work for several months a year in mines, forests, quarries, where they were treated almost like slaves. The prophets began to look with disfavor on Solomon's political and religious life. He was criticized by some people for the extravagance that made life harder for his people. Solomon seemed to forget that he had once written, "How much better it is to get wisdom than to get gold."

Worse yet, he let his wives influence him. Many of these women prayed to the moon or to gods called Baal or Moloch. First his wives wanted idols. Then they wanted priests, altars, shrines. Solomon gave them everything they asked. He even took part in their strange forms of worship.

After Solomon had broken both the first and second commandments, the Lord said to him, "Forasmuch as thou hast not kept my statutes, I will surely rend the kingdom from thee. Notwithstanding in thy days I will not do it for David thy father's sake; but I will rend it out of the hand of thy son."

Soon after that, Hadad, an Edomite prince, rebelled and cut off a slice of Solomon's kingdom. A group of outlaws broke away. Jeroboam, one of Solomon's officials, who was industrious and a man of valor, won a following of men who no longer wanted Solomon as their king. But when Solomon found out, Jeroboam had to flee to Egypt to escape from the king's anger.

Solomon continued to do many things right, but wealth and intellect alone couldn't maintain the kingdom. So long as he worshiped the one true God, things had gone well. Israel had come to the peak of her prosperity. For almost forty years, Solomon and his country were strong. He gave Israel good government, beautiful buildings, a thriving trade and commerce, peaceful relations with other countries.

His countless wise sayings lived after him, including the youthful plea, "Give therefore thy servant an understanding heart . . . that I may discern between good and bad."

But his turning to material worship eventually led to the destruction of the kingdom.

The story is found in I Kings, chapters 2 through 11.

NEHEMIAH

The kings who ruled Judah and
Israel after Solomon died were sometimes
weak and unwise. From about 922 B.C. on,
Elijah, Elisha, Isaiah, Jeremiah, and other
prophets were often the real leaders.

In 721 B.C. the Assyrians conquered Samaria,
the capital of Israel. About two centuries later the
Chaldeans took over Jerusalem, the capital of Judah.
Finally all of what is now called the
Middle East came under the control of Persia.
The Persian king, Cyrus the Great, declared
that all captive people could go back
to their homelands.

So some people returned to Jerusalem in
Judah. Not all of the Jews there were happy to
have people returning. It was hard to make a
living, and the Samaritans were hostile. Worst
of all, Jerusalem's walls still had not been repaired. The
Jews felt neglected
and weak, unsure how to go about
establishing their nationhood.

163

A BOLD PLAN

Nehemiah served in the palace of Artaxerxes, king of Persia. As cupbearer, Nehemiah had almost as many privileges as a prince. He wore elegant clothes and ate royal food. But he knew many of his people, the Jews in Jerusalem, had almost nothing.

One day Hanani and some fellow Jews came from Judah to the winter palace of Artaxerxes at Shushan. Nehemiah talked with them. "How are things with the people still in Jerusalem?" he asked. "And how are the exiles who went back there?"

Hanani shook his head sadly. "Things are not good," he said. "The walls of Jerusalem are broken down. The gates are burned."

"The people have a hard life," added another one of the visitors.

Nehemiah knew that when a city had no walls, enemies could make frequent raids. People lived in fear that they would lose crops, houses, even their lives. It was bad enough for any city to be in ruins. But Jerusalem had been the capital city of the Jews, and still was the holy city where people had come to learn about God.

When Nehemiah heard these words, he sat down and wept, and then he fasted. He also began to pray.

In his prayers Nehemiah confessed that his people had disobeyed God. As a result, Judah, their kingdom, had been destroyed and the people scattered into captivity. But Nehemiah remembered that the Lord told Moses that if the people turned to God and kept His Commandments, they would be brought back to His chosen place.

Nehemiah wanted to help the Jews in Jerusalem. Anything he could do he was willing to do.

For a long time Nehemiah prayed about what action to take. Then the answer came. Why couldn't he go to Jerusalem and help rebuild the wall? He was full of plans. But Nehemiah couldn't find courage to ask the king to let him leave the palace long enough to help with the wall. It might take months.

Finally Nehemiah felt he must not wait any longer. He prayed, "O Lord, please help me when I ask the king for a great favor. Let him be merciful toward me."

Then one day when Nehemiah was with the king and queen, Artaxerxes asked: "Why are you looking so sad? You're not sick, so this must be sorrow in your heart."

The king's question frightened Nehemiah. A cupbearer was never supposed to look anxious or worried. Had he made the king angry? And if he told him what he wanted, would he be even more angry?

"Let the king live forever," Nehemiah said politely. "Why shouldn't I be sad? The city of my ancestors is in ruins."

"What do you want done?" asked Artaxerxes.

"If it please the king," Nehemiah said, "send me to Judah to rebuild the city of my fathers."

Artaxerxes asked, "How long will you be gone? And when will you come back?" They agreed on a time.

Nehemiah knew that on his journey he would have to travel through places where governors appointed to serve the Persian king might be unfriendly to travelers.

"Could letters be given to governors beyond the Euphrates River?" he asked. "Then they will let me go through their regions on the way to Judah."

The king nodded in agreement. By then Nehemiah had another thought. He would need wood for making gates, for part of the wall, and for a house to live in. Not many trees grew around Jerusalem.

Only the stories he had heard of the sufferings of his people gave Nehemiah courage to ask, "And a letter to Asaph, keeper of the king's forest. If he could give me timber . . ."

Artaxerxes gave Nehemiah everything he asked for— permission to get timber, a leave from his job as cup-bearer, letters to the governors. The king also appointed him temporary governor of Judah.

When Nehemiah was ready to begin the journey, the king sent captains of the army and horsemen to go with him. Nehemiah set off full of hope and thanksgiving for God's goodness.

As they got close to Jerusalem, they met with unfriend-liness. Samaritans under the leadership of Sanballat wanted the city to stay weak. Sanballat feared that a rebuilt Jerusalem might threaten Samaria and the position he held as governor under Persian rule. He didn't want any leader coming in who might help the Jews become strong. But because Nehemiah had letters from Arta-xerxes, no one dared stop him.

So after many weeks, Nehemiah finally arrived in

Jerusalem. He saw heaps of rock where the wall should have been. Nehemiah entered the city through gates that hung loose and were blackened by fire. Tangles of thistles grew everywhere. Fewer people lived there than Nehemiah expected, and they were very poor. A long time before, they had rebuilt the temple. But Xerxes I, one of the Persian kings, had commanded them not to repair the wall.

For three days Nehemiah rested and prayed. He did not talk to the rulers, nobles, priests, or workmen. Before he told the people he had come to help them rebuild, he wanted to have a plan. The wisdom to lead the people would come from God.

On the third night, Nehemiah took a few servants outside the city with him to see exactly what needed to be done. Nehemiah rode a donkey, but in some places because of stones and rubbish he had to walk. Some of the wall was intact, but most was now heaps of stones too broken to be reused.

Nehemiah went by moonlight from the gate of the valley in the west to the south, then east and north to see all the wall that was broken down. Jackals yapped nearby. An owl screeched.

As he rode back into the city, Nehemiah knew he could trust God. God had sent him here. There would be supplies when needed, and people to do the work.

Next morning, Nehemiah called together the rulers, priests, nobles, and workmen. Then he said, "You see the trouble we are in. Come and let us build up the wall of Jerusalem."

Nehemiah then told them that King Artaxerxes of Persia had let him come and had even provided wood for rebuilding the gates. He also spoke about his

conviction of God's help. Nehemiah's trust, courage, and strong purpose made the people eager to start.

"Let us build!" someone shouted. Others took up the cry. No one knew better than Nehemiah that building the wall would take skill, hard work, and cooperation. But he and his people could do it, if they would trust and obey God.

PLOTS, PROTECTION, AND A WALL

Nehemiah didn't waste time getting started on rebuilding the wall around Jerusalem. He first asked the people to clear away everything that would hinder the building. To do this, some women worked alongside the men. They saved good stones for use in the new wall.

Soon the sound of saws, mallets, and hammers echoed through the city. Priests, merchants, nobles, worked side by side. Many families repaired the section of the wall closest to their homes. Carpenters made gates.

Enemies of the Jews were furious when they saw the wall going up. Hot-tempered Sanballat was jealous of Nehemiah's position and the help he was getting from Artaxerxes.

"What are these feeble Jews doing?" Sanballat jeered when he spoke to the Samaritan army. "Will they make a wall out of rubbish?"

Tobiah, governor of the Ammonites, said the wall was so weak that, if a fox jumped on it, it would tumble down!

Nehemiah heard what was said, but he kept on praying. His energy and faith spurred the others on. The wall did not tumble down. It got stronger every day.

171

When insults failed to stop the work, Sanballat and Tobiah switched to a plan of causing confusion, or even using force.

"Our enemies plot to attack us," warned Jews living outside the city.

"You don't have to be afraid," Nehemiah told the workers. "Remember the Lord and fight for your brethren, your sons and daughters, your wives, and your houses."

Then Nehemiah asked each worker to wear a sword at his side and keep other weapons within reach. Half of the men worked while half of them stood guard. Jews living outside Jerusalem moved into the city. A trumpeter stayed by Nehemiah ready to blast out a signal at any sign of attack. "God will fight for us," Nehemiah said.

Now the builders worked harder and faster than ever. Up at dawn, they often kept working even after the stars were out. Day and night they kept guard on the wall. Nehemiah himself slept only a few hours each night. Neither he nor his servants or guardsmen took their clothes off, except for washing. Nehemiah knew that if he and the others were obedient to God, they would get the wall built before the enemy attacked.

Nehemiah's faith and patience were tested not only by threats from his enemies but by problems with his own people. Some were jealous of Nehemiah. A few workmen didn't do their share. Others doubted that the work could be done. One day the people came to Nehemiah and said, "There is too much rubbish. We are not able to build the wall."

In the midst of discouragement and danger, Nehemiah encouraged everyone to keep on. Patient and wise, he never stopped trusting God.

Because people were working on the wall instead of looking after their fields and gardens, food became scarce. And with no crops to sell, farmers lacked money. They fell behind in paying their taxes. Some of the Jews lent money to their own people so they could pay their taxes to Persia. Then people came to Nehemiah with sad stories. "Rich Jews have seized our vineyards, grain, even our houses because we couldn't pay back what we borrowed, plus the interest."

"We are their brothers, and our children are just like theirs," added another. "Yet we must sell our children into slavery to get money to live."

These reports and others made Nehemiah angry. As governor, he himself had a right to collect taxes. Instead, he had lent money and given grain to the poor. He had invited those who were hungry to eat at his table.

Nehemiah called a meeting of landowners and officials. "Those of us who came from Shushan have done all we could to help our Jewish brothers who are in need," he said. "You are forcing them into slavery worse than they knew in exile."

The men sat silent and ashamed.

"What you are doing is evil," Nehemiah scolded. "You shouldn't give our enemies reason to criticize us."

Nehemiah then told the men to give back the fields, vineyards, grain, and houses they had seized. "Drop your claims," he demanded.

Admitting they had been wrong, the officials promised, "We will do as you say." They agreed to help instead of trying to get rich. And they would no longer force other people's children to become slaves!

Nehemiah went back to wall building.

Afraid that an assault at that time might end in failure,

Nehemiah's enemies pretended that they wanted to work with him in peace. Sanballat, Tobiah, and their friend, the Arab named Geshem, sent a message reading, "Come, let us meet together in some one of the villages on the plain of Ono."

Nehemiah knew they intended to harm him, possibly to kill him. He didn't lack courage, but he wasn't going to walk into a trap. He had come to get the wall built. Nothing could stand in his way.

He sent back the message, "I am doing a great work. Why should I stop and come down to you?"

Four times they sent the same message. Nehemiah kept giving the same answer.

The fifth time, Sanballat sent a servant with a threat. "It is reported that the Jews are planning to revolt, and that you intend to make yourself king. I am going to report this to Artaxerxes. Come and talk this over with me."

Nehemiah had no such plan. "The things you say are not true," he answered. "You are inventing them."

Although what Sanballat was saying was a lie, Nehemiah would be in trouble if the king believed Sanballat. Again Nehemiah turned to God. "O God, strengthen my hands," he prayed.

Several days later he went to the house of Shemaiah, the son of a priest. He had been there only a few minutes when his host clutched at the sleeve of Nehemiah's robe.

"Let us hide in the temple and bolt the door," said Shemaiah. "Your enemies are hunting for you. Tonight they will come to kill you."

If Nehemiah hid in the temple because of fear, the people would see him as a coward. No longer would they be willing to have him as their leader. Besides that, only priests had the right to enter the temple. Nehemiah was

GLOSSARY

Ark—also called *Ark of the Covenant.*
A chest made of acacia wood containing the tablets of
stone on which the Ten Commandments were carved. The
Israelites carried the ark on poles as they traveled.

Baal

The name of the fertility god of the Canaanites. Their
farmers believed worship of Baal would bring fertility to
crops and livestock. Some Israelites, as they settled in the
Promised Land, adopted Baal worship.

Israelites

Descendants of Israel (Jacob); also called Hebrews. They
considered themselves to be a "chosen" people who had a
covenant obligation to serve the one God and obey His
laws, and in turn they would receive God's protection and
deliverance from evil.

Marriage

In early Old Testament times a man's wife was often se-
lected for him by his father, or other head of the family.
Many men had only one wife. But it was neither uncom-
mon nor unacceptable to have several wives. In a society

where flocks and herds meant wealth it was an advantage to have a number of children, especially sons, to tend them and to carry on the family traditions.

Names

A name was chosen very carefully. It was supposed to represent some characteristic of the person or an event connected with his or her birth. On rare or specific occasions, after a person did something unusual or changed in thought or character, he or she would receive a new name.

See Jacob to Israel, page 35.

Passover

A celebration commemorating the beginning of the Israelites' freedom after years of slavery in Egypt. At time of Passover people were to eat lamb, unleavened bread, and bitter herbs.

Sacrifice

In Old Testament times many people thought God would be pleased by gifts. To win favor, to show obedience, and to express thanks, they offered oil, the firstfruits of their crops, their best animals, and other cherished possessions. Sacrifices were made frequently. The arrival of an honored guest in one's home or reaching an important agreement might be accompanied by making an offering to God. Festivals, marriages, and the crowning of a king were celebrated by offering a sacrifice.

Women

In Old Testament times women were considered inferior to men. They were supposed to be a "help-meet" for their husbands, managing household affairs and bearing children. Virtuous, active wives were valued. A woman with no sons had no status in the community. Women had considerable liberty. They mingled with men in their separate duties and played a part in public celebrations. Sometimes they became leaders or held public office. Deborah, for example, was a judge whose functions included both civil and military leadership.

Writing

The written word was being used centuries before Abraham's time. Messages were inscribed on clay, wood, metal, and stone. Later, strips of papyrus, parchment, or leather were used. These were called scrolls. The reader unrolled the scroll with one hand and rolled it up again with the other as he read the message.

DO YOU KNOW?

ABRAHAM

1. In what way was Abraham a pioneer?
2. What promises did God make to Abraham? Gen. 17: 1-8.
3. Abraham was generous with Lot, offering him the choice land. How could he do this and still have no feeling of loss?
4. What did Abraham learn about God at the time he was going to sacrifice Isaac?
5. Can we talk with God the way Abraham did?
6. In what way was Abraham's concept of God different from that of most of his countrymen? How does it differ from yours?

JACOB

1. What was the result of Jacob's deceiving his father, Isaac, and stealing his brother's blessing?
2. How does being honest affect your relationship to your family, friends, and God?

183

3. Jacob had a dream at Bethel in which he saw angels going up and down a ladder. What did this dream mean?

4. How did Jacob gain independence for himself and his family?

5. Jacob did not become a better person all of a sudden. What were some of the steps in his progress?

6. Jacob wrestled with his thoughts and prayed all night at Peniel. What does his experience show us about how we can resolve problems at home, at school, and on the playground?

7. Considering their earlier relationship, how could Jacob and Esau have such a happy reunion?

8. What problems do you see in the story of Jacob that are still problems today?

9. What changes took place in Jacob's character from the time he left Beersheba until he returned?

JOSEPH

1. Joseph's relationship with his family changes completely from the beginning to the end of his life. How would you describe his brothers' attitude toward him when he was a teen-ager at home? What was Joseph's attitude toward them when the family was reunited in Egypt?

2. What was Joseph's attitude toward Potiphar? His fellow prisoners? The pharaoh? Egyptian people? God?

3. It is easy to say that it was because of prayer that Joseph was brought out of prison to an important position. But, what is prayer? What do you think Joseph's prayer might have been?

4. Why did Joseph become so popular with the Egyptians?

5. Judah had been the one who urged his brothers to sell Joseph into slavery. How did his plea to Joseph in Egypt show how much he had changed? Gen. 44:18-34.
6. Joseph not only forgave his brothers but saw a higher purpose in what had happened. What was that purpose? Gen. 45:5.

MOSES

1. At the time he saw the burning bush, Moses claimed he was slow of speech and lacked confidence as a leader. What examples can you give to show that he overcame these limitations? How was he able to overcome them?
2. What plan of government did Jethro suggest to Moses? Ex. 18:13-26. How was this plan similar to what we call democracy today?
3. What do the Ten Commandments have to say about our relationship to God? Our relationship to others?
4. What differences do you see between the Commandments as listed in Exodus 20 and Deuteronomy 5?
5. Why are the Commandments as important to us today as they were for the people of Moses' time?
6. Why did the Israelites have to spend such a long time in the wilderness?
7. What do you think was the most important thing Moses did for the Israelites?

JOSHUA

1. What had Joshua done before he took over as leader that prepared him for the position?
2. When the children of Israel crossed into Canaan, what experiences did they have that were similar to those when they left Egypt?

3. During the time Joshua was their leader, the Israelites extended their territory a great deal. What was Joshua's attitude toward occupying the enemy's land?
4. What activities or statements show how Joshua thought about God?
5. Joshua obeyed God as he understood Him, but he still had some mistaken ideas about God. Can you pick out some of these in his farewell speech? Josh. 23:15; Josh. 24:19, 20.

RUTH

1. Why did Ruth decide to leave her homeland and go with Naomi?
2. What qualities did Ruth express?
3. What proof did Ruth have of God's care?
4. What problems did Ruth have that are also problems today?

SAMUEL

1. How did Samuel show, even as a child, that he was good at listening and obeying?
2. How did Samuel gain the respect and trust of the Israelites?
3. Why did the Israelites want a king? What were Samuel's arguments against it?
4. What were some of Samuel's weaknesses? His strengths?
5. What does it mean to be a prophet? Are you a prophet?

DAVID

1. Why was David unafraid when he went out to meet Goliath? What does that say to us about the way we can conquer fears?

2. Jonathan and David stayed best friends for many years. What qualities did each of them have that made the friendship strong and lasting?
3. How did David show that he was humble enough to take good advice even though he was the leader? I Sam. 25:18-35.
4. Give examples of times when David showed love for his enemies.
5. Although basically good, David sometimes did wrong things. How did his mistakes bring suffering to him and his nation?
6. How did David rebuild his life and his kingdom after his exile?
7. What experiences prepared David for the kingship?
8. What gifts did David leave for Solomon and for the people?

SOLOMON

1. In what ways did Solomon show wisdom?
2. How did Solomon fall short of what he might have been?
3. Which of the Ten Commandments did Solomon break?
4. Why did the people feel more awe than love for Solomon?
5. How does this story relate to conditions today?
6. What are proverbs? Find three that especially appeal to you.

NEHEMIAH

1. What qualities did Nehemiah have that are important for any leader to possess?

2. Why was Nehemiah able to get the people to work at building the wall when they hadn't been willing to work at it before?
3. Why did the enemies of the Jews try to stop Nehemiah from building the wall? Why weren't they successful in their attempts?
4. When an attack seemed likely, Nehemiah armed his men with swords and spears. Why did they never have to use them?
5. The wall Nehemiah and the others built around Jerusalem was of stone and wood. But Nehemiah felt that Jerusalem and he were protected by a different kind of wall. What was their protection? How can we build such a wall?

Abraham

Joseph

Jacob

Moses

Joshua

1750 B.C.   1600 B.C.

1300 B.C.

STORY TIME-LINE